miracles
do happen

The POWER and PLACE
of MIRACLES as a SIGN
to the WORLD

WAYNE T. JACKSON

Destiny Image® Publishers, Inc.
P.O. Box 310
Shippensburg, PA 17257-0310

*"Speaking to the Purposes of God for This Generation
and for the Generations to Come"*

ISBN 0-7684-2261-2

For Worldwide Distribution
Printed in the U.S.A.

This book and all other Destiny Image, Revival Press, MercyPlace,
Fresh Bread, Destiny Image Fiction, and Treasure House books are available
at Christian bookstores and distributors worldwide.

1 2 3 4 5 6 7 8 9 10 / 10 09 08 07 06 05

For a U.S. bookstore nearest you, call
1-800-722-6774.

For more information on foreign distributors, call
717-532-3040.

Or reach us on the Internet:
www.destinyimage.com

Acknowledgments

I would like to thank my Lord and Savior Jesus Christ for giving me the opportunity to share His Word through this book. To my wife, Beverly Y. Jackson for her many years of love, support, encouragement, and prayer. To my father, the late Horace Jackson, and my mother, Willie Mae, for instilling in me the fear of God and the importance of a personal relationship with Him. To my loving children, Wayne Timothy, and his wife, Carla; Shontel Michelle Maple and her husband, Andrew; Dominique Yvonne; Royal Wayne; Brandon Timothy; Jubilee Hosanna Praise; and Haven Christianna. You continue to inspire me as I see God's hand working in each of your lives. To my father in the ministry, the late Royal T. Bozeman, and his wife, Corinne Bozeman, for teaching me to live by faith. Finally, to Pastor Aaron D. Lewis for his editorial input.

Endorsements

"Yes! I believe—and experience—that *MIRACLES DO HAPPEN*. I believe Bishop Wayne Jackson's (for right now miracles in each of our lives) book will stir your heart and... release your faith for the miracles you've been waiting on. Take it into your heart and body and be delivered!

Dr. Oral Roberts
Founder, Oral Roberts University
Author, *Still Doing the Impossible*

Table of Contents

Preface

*WHY MIRACLES HAVE
BECOME MY LIFE'S PASSION*

Although it has been years since I have been set free from the bonds of heroin addiction, if I just close my eyes right now, I can clearly remember the trauma that I endured that nearly cost me my life. It all started early on, when I was thirteen years old. I remember seeing all kinds of colors and shades of fresh beautiful flowers everywhere. People came from far and wide to pay their final respects to my father. I remember feeling somewhat mortified as I gazed at my father while he lay dead in a casket, patiently waiting to be eulogized.

I had never in my life seen my father so lifeless. During his lifetime, my dad was the kind of man who made everyone feel so alive and so good about themselves. Now he just lay there, unable to smile, speak, or know what was going on. At that moment it began to dawn on me that my daddy was gone, and he wasn't coming back. The reality of that thought hit me hard, like a blunt object to the head.

For the rest of my life I would have to live without the guidance, direction, and love of my father. In my newly-teenaged mind I just could not understand why God would allow my father to die when he was the greatest man and example that I have ever seen. Simply put, daddy was my hero. Not only was he a hero to me, but also to the parishioners that he pastored. My father was a pastor of a church in the Pentecostal Assemblies of the World *denomination* in the small town of Wayne, Michigan, where I was raised.

Truly, everyone that knew him and even everyone that came across his path immediately sensed the Spirit and compassion of Jesus Christ working on the inside of my father. My dad was the kind of man that would literally give you the shirt off of his back. And often he did just that. When I was small, I remember watching my dad help people who were helpless and needy.

So in my adolescent mind I thought that if anyone should live forever and escape the jaws of death, he should surely deserve that honor. After all, he loved people and that was what Jesus Christ called us to do. Honestly, I just could not understand why God picked my dad over so many other worthy candidates that I thought deserved to die more than he did.

I'd known people even in the church who were just evil and wicked people that still had a lease on life. I couldn't understand it. They gossiped all of the time and would often backbite. Some folks kept trouble stirring all of the time, and they were still alive to cause more trouble. Why didn't God kill out all the notorious thieves and robbers in the world? Let's face it; they probably wouldn't even be surprised by a suddenly shortened life, considering the reckless lives they chose to lead. Sudden death would feel right for them; at least I thought so.

Added to the people that I personally knew that I thought deserved death more than my dad did, were the thousands of murderers that were still alive, planning their next hit that would ultimately kill off thousands of innocent people. They still had a chance to enjoy life, however they perceived enjoyment. All kinds of questions started to arise in my mind. Whether they were or not, I sincerely thought that each question was as legitimate as could be. Why would God allow the drug dealers to live freely even though they were responsible for filling children's veins with drugs and guilty of destroying so many families? They got to live, but my father, a respected man who gave himself wholeheartedly to the work of the Lord, had to die of an aneurysm.

I couldn't seem to shake it. For the life of me I could not stop thinking about it. The more that I continued to ponder it I got mad, awfully mad. Far worse than my feelings of anger was the fact that these thoughts began to breed fast-budding seeds of bitterness in my heart. It would have been bad enough if I held bitterness in my heart against a person. Most Christians would agree that harboring bitter feelings alone would have tremendously slowed my progress in life.

My problem was far more severe. I was actually bitter with God. I was mad at God. Consider that—mad at God and unable to do anything about it. No matter how loud I screamed or how intensely I cried it wouldn't seem to affect God. Since I did not get any answers, I began to believe that God killed my dad or at least allowed him to be taken from us, and there was no way that I could get back at God for doing that. In my adolescent mind I sort of thought that God planned this hit on my dad.

Up until that point in my young life, I had heard quite a few messages from preachers and traveling evangelists. However, I really did not understand the great negative impact that housing bitterness within my heart could actually cause. I did not realize then that harboring bitter thoughts and having a bitter spirit could actually hinder my progress in life. Little did I understand that bitterness would eventually lead me toward a path of destruction. Bitterness was causing me to quickly go downward in more ways than one without me even realizing it. If only I had known.

*Pursue peace with all **people**, and holiness, without which no one will see the Lord: looking carefully lest anyone fall short of the grace of God; lest any root of bitterness* *springing up cause trouble, and by this many become defiled* (Heb. 12:14-15, emphasis added).

Growing up in Pentecostalism, I can't even count how many times I heard Hebrews 12:14 quoted or preached on. If I got a quarter for every time that I heard that scripture referenced, I'd have been rich a long time ago. All Pentecostals in my background adopted this particular verse as their theme scripture. Us "sanctified" folks used this verse to separate us from all of the other church folks that we called nominal saints.

The problem with the love affair with this scripture is that they actually misquoted the verse. In a conscientious effort to promote moral living in the church, they would single out the middle portion of the scripture, "Holiness without which no one will see the Lord." Although this phrase is obviously within the Scriptures, it is not the only message therein. Not knowing what the rest of Scripture says can be dangerous and even promote heretical teachings.

According to this verse, the Bible actually instructs believers to do two things that will guarantee that they will see the Lord. The first thing it says is to pursue peace with all people. In other words, Christian brothers and sisters do not have God's permission to cause confusion among one another, or to live contentiously. At all costs the child of God should do everything within their power to promote peace, not only within the church, but also in society. Although they may not have realized it, most Christians were failing miserably in this area.

AFTER YOU HAVE ACCOMPLISHED LIVING IN PEACE WITH GOD'S PEOPLE, THEN YOU MUST PURSUE HOLINESS, WHICH IS SIMPLY THE CHARACTER OF GOD.

There were so many Christians when I was a child who thought it was their God-given charge to feud and to live their lives quarreling with other believers over doctrinal issues, failing to adhere to God's command to live peaceably. The truth is, you can't skip over peace and jump to holiness. One precedes the other. After you have accomplished living in peace with God's people, then you must pursue holiness, which is simply the character of God.

When you really think about it, it only makes good sense. Peace and God's character always go hand in hand. They are somewhat inseparable. But then the next scripture says some very important things that are worth mentioning also. It says, "lest any root of bitterness springing up cause trouble, and by this many become defiled." That is the part that I rarely if ever heard taught. If that lesson was taught, I surely did not remember it being taught.

I really did not understand as a young teenaged boy that my bitterness would cause me to become corrupted beyond belief. Corrupt is exactly what I became. I had to learn the hard way that what you refuse to release would inevitably stay bottled up on the inside of you until something else causes you to release. Usually that "something else" is a counterfeit thing. Mad at God, believing that He killed my father, and not knowing how to properly channel all of my anger, I began to look for areas to release.

For three years I felt like a bottle of root beer, rapidly shaken back and forth. I had bottled up within me many mixed emotions about God, my dad's premature death, church folks, and church in general. I just could not get a real grasp on everything that was happening, nor was anyone offering any real help. So for the next three years, this seed of bitterness not only took deep root in my soul, but it also eventually sprung up to become a tall tree, one that only God could cut down.

When I was sixteen I decided to give up on the whole church scene and began to experiment with the world. Unlike others who flirted with the church and the world simultaneously, I did not want to have anything to do with God or His Church anymore. I felt that if I were going to be a sinner, I might as well be a full-fledged one and not half-step. I felt as if God betrayed me, so I opened myself up to the world, believing that this was my big chance to even the score between God and me.

As I said, much of my beginnings were experimental. I was reared as a pastor's child and was not exposed to the things like drugs and alcohol. All of those things were new to me. I did not start out taking hard drugs. The hard stuff came later down the road. Like many first-time users, I had to ease into their new territory, taking one step at a time.

It started with what the people in the streets call the "small stuff," marijuana, also known as reefer. King Solomon once said, "Catch us the foxes, The little foxes that spoil the vines, For our vines *have* tender grapes" (Song of Sol. 2:15, emphasis added). According to this verse, the little foxes, not the big ones, destroyed the vines. That leads me to believe that, by the time the big foxes get to the vines, they'll already be ruined. It was the so-called "little drug," marijuana, that exposed me to the world of drugs. It eventually led me to far more dangerous and addictive drugs that would eventually get me strung out and yes, ruined.

So, for a couple of years, I used marijuana as my primary choice for getting high. For me it was initially a great escape. As with anything that you use long enough, you eventually get accustomed to it. When that happens, your body naturally begins to call out for stronger substances that are able to produce results quicker, with more bells and whistles so to speak. That's when heroin became my friend. No one in the world could have convinced me of just how addictive and destructive heroin could actually become.

Of the smorgasbord of the drugs available, heroin is perhaps the most deceptive and addictive drug of all. Coupled with the addiction are the horrific consequences that follow. After prolonged use of heroin, your veins become scarred. At times your veins will actually collapse. You can contract bacterial infections in your blood vessels and your heart valves. Heroin weakens your lungs, often causing pneumonia and tuberculosis. On the street, drug dealers add all kinds of foreign substances to heroin to try to increase its effectiveness and potency.

These additives are rarely soluble and tend to clog the blood vessels that lead to vital organs such as the lungs, liver, the kidneys, and the brain. This in turn can incite fast spreading infections or even death in clusters of cells inside your vital organs. Some people develop immune reactions to these additives and other contaminants, which produces arthritis and other hematological problems.

Since heroin addiction is often a group thing, sharing injection equipment is very common. And when fluids cross and are exchanged it can lead to some of the most severe cases of heroin abuse-infections with hepatitis B and C, HIV, and a myriad of blood-borne viruses. After one has contracted these diseases, they can be passed on through sexual intercourse or less physical contact. This is just a short list of the horrible price that the body has to pay just to get high off of heroin.

When the dealer on the street sells you the drug, he never gives you a written disclosure statement with all of the details of the side effects of this so-called "wonder drug." The dealers know that once you get hooked, you are usually hooked for life unless God supernaturally intervenes on your behalf. So, for the next three years I was reduced to absolutely nothing. I became someone that I was not. There was almost nothing that I would not do to satisfy my inner cravings.

At first I felt so ashamed of myself, knowing that I was raised with such higher standards than I was demonstrating. But, after a while, nothing mattered to me apart from getting my high. Although I truly loved my family and did not desire to cause them any harm, I would steal from them just to get a hit. In time,

I became so ruthless that my priorities totally centered on getting high. Everything that I did was based on my next fix.

Not realizing it, I was being controlled by a demon spirit. My family and friends were pushed over into second and third position to what I thought was my dearest friend, heroin. And when I say friend, that is literally what heroin became to me, my best friend. Heroin was always faithfully there when I needed it. In fact, there was a time when I did not even care whether I was dead or alive, as long as heroin was with me.

I wasn't the only person that this drug had such demonic control over. There were many others who thought just as irrationally as I did. The very nature of this drug seems to make one delusional. And when that happens, you begin to believe things that are totally untrue, unreal, and impossible in the most negative sense. That is why it tends to be so hard to break free from this awful addiction on your own.

You start believing that you are bigger than life itself. Although everything around you proves that you are really on the bottom of the dunghill, that doesn't matter. The addiction makes you want more and it seems like a never-ending cycle. Unfortunately, for some, the only way out is death. The ones who choose death's dreadful path have not sought the spirit of God for help and, as a result, they falsely believe that there is no hope.

The following account appeared some years ago in an Ann Landers column. It is a heartbreaker, entitled, "King Heroin Is My Shepherd, I Shall Always Want." I could instantly tell from reading the poem that this young lady may have had some exposure to the Church and the things of God at some point in her life. These heartbreaking words were part of a twisted paraphrase of the beloved 23rd Psalm, found in a car with the body of a 23-year-old young woman, near Reidsville, North Carolina. Her death was ruled a suicide from a hookup with the car's exhaust pipe. It is very interesting how her poem starkly contrasts the 23rd Psalm.

The actual 23rd Psalm (KJV) reads:

The Lord is my shepherd; I shall not want. He maketh me to lie down in green pastures: he leadeth me beside the still waters. He restoreth my soul: he leadeth me in the paths of righteousness for his name's sake. Yea, though I walk through the valley of the shadow of death, I will fear no evil: for thou art with me; thy rod and thy staff they comfort me. Thou preparest a table before me in the presence of mine enemies: thou anointest my head with oil; my cup runneth over. Surely goodness and mercy shall follow me all the days of my life: and I will dwell in the house of the Lord forever.

In dark contrast, her note read:

"King Heroin is my shepherd, I shall always want. He maketh me to lie down in the gutters. He leadeth me beside the troubled waters. He destroyeth my soul. He leadeth me in the paths of wickedness. Yea, I shall walk through the valley of poverty and will fear no evil for thou, Heroin, art with me. Thy needle and thy capsule comfort me. Thou strippest the table of groceries in the presence of my family. Thou robbest my head of reason. My cup of sorrow runneth over. Surely heroin addiction shall stalk me all the days of my life and I will dwell in the house of the damned forever."

After reading this depressing poem, I could personally relate to how real this experience actually was for her. My addiction lasted for about five years, from the time I was 18 until I turned 23 years old. During that time, I heavily used heroin and cocaine. The drugs became my replacement for food. In fact, drugs were my food. At one point, I had loss so much weight that I literally went down to skin and bones. I was a fully-grown adult weighing 105 pounds. I was smaller than most women who wore dress sizes in between four and six.

Like a vagabond, I was living from place to place. Pretty much anywhere I would lay my head is where I would stay for the night. Many of my family members had become very intolerant because of my behavior and didn't want me staying in their homes. They knew that I was a thief and could not be trusted. Everyone pretty much cast me out of their inner and outer circles. For the most, part everyone gave up on me. In many ways I gave up on myself. No one wanted me to be around except for...

My mother has always been a praying woman. Even though the enemy brought me down so low, my mother was committed to continue to love me throughout my entire process. As a word of encouragement to any mothers who are reading this book whose child has been attacked by the devil in one way or another, never stop praying for your child. I understand and respect that there has to be a line drawn when it comes to other things such as lending and giving them money freely.

Better than anyone else, I know that you have to show tough love at times. However, under no circumstances should you ever give up hope. For as long as I can remember, my mother has always practiced living a prayerful and fasted lifestyle. She knew that if all else failed, prayer would certainly work. My condition got to a point when I became so bad and caught out on drugs, that my mother decided to go on a forty day fast, believing that God would break this addiction off of my life.

I had lost all hope, and no one who personally knew me ever believed that I would be free. For the most part, everybody thought that I would be shot and killed or overdose on drugs. My family and friends confessed that they believed that at any moment they were going to receive a phone call announcing that I was found somewhere dead. I really did not have anyone in my family whom I could turn to at the time for strength.

Two of my brothers were on drugs just like I was. My other brother was a drug dealer. I knew that they couldn't help me since they were as bad off as I was. My dealing brother viewed me in the same way that he would all of his clients, as another customer. However, my sisters did not sit idly by, just watching this happen. They would often come to the drug houses and pull my brothers and me out against our will. Despite their sincere efforts, I was still trapped.

I've always believed that at some point in a person's life, they will have a life-defining moment. What I mean by that is a point in life where you begin to look at where you are right now and carefully evaluate your life. Like a skilled medical practitioner, you then look at the prognosis for your life and consider whether or not it's even worth the fight. At this point you have to make a decision to either make massive changes or die the way you are.

At 23 years old, I was sentenced to jail for suspicion of breaking and entry. That was my life-defining moment. There are many people who view jail as the worst place on earth to be. And that may be true for some, but for many others it is the only place where God can actually speak to you. When you are living life in the fast lane it can be almost impossible to hear the message of Christ in the midst of wheeling and dealing and street hustling. But in jail God has you cornered. And that's a good thing.

While I was in my jail cell, I remember God giving me an ultimatum. I clearly remember Him telling me that I would serve Him and have life or I would die. He really didn't leave many options for multiple choice. He left that choice clearly up to me. For whatever reason, I knew that this time was different than any other time. I felt like I came face to face with my destiny.

I sensed deeply within that I had to surrender my life to Jesus. Deep within, I believed that if I did not surrender my life to Him I would have died for sure. The problem was that my addiction was so strong and many others had told me that kicking the habit would be virtually impossible. Other addicts voiced, "You may kick the habit for a while but it will come back eventually. If not in weeks or months, it'll be back in a couple of years or so." Although those words were ultra-discouraging, I knew that God was more powerful than my addiction. I believed that if anyone could break the bonds of this spirit from me, only God could do it. It was at that point that the Word of God that I heard as a child began to quicken within my spirit.

> *"Jesus said to him, 'If you can believe, all things **are** possible to him who believes'"* (Mark 9:23).

On the streets, they called heroin the king. But I began to realize that Jesus was the King of kings and that he had the power to take this compulsion totally away from me. "And He has on His robe and on His thigh a name written: KING OF KINGS AND LORD OF LORDS" (Rev. 19:16). When I was released from jail I didn't go looking for a fix like most of the brothers do after they are released. I wanted to find a church, and that is exactly what I did.

I went to Faith Apostolic Temple where Elder Royal T. Bozeman was the Pastor, and gave my heart to fully to Jesus. I was desperately searching for something better than I had ever experienced. What attracted me to this church was the fact that it was not a traditional church in terms external holiness. There were many young people who were serious about God there. Elder Bozeman was a great man, anointed by God, who taught the principles of faith. He took me in as his son. He never held my past addictions against me in any way. In fact, he never really mentioned it. Pastor Bozeman saw in the spirit what God could do with my life and that's what his entire focus was on.

Years later, I married his daughter Beverly, who is the love of my life. After Elder Bozeman died, I became the succeeding pastor of Faith Apostolic Temple, which is now known as Great Faith Ministries. But it was here that I began to learn about the principles of believing God for everything from staying clean to purchasing the things that I needed in life to building a great church for God.

I had faith in God to know that I could be delivered. Instantly, God delivered me from heroin. I am not being critical of other methods of becoming free. I am only bragging about the one that worked for me, the HGM (Holy Ghost Method). That is one of the reasons that I don't believe in terms like "recovering drug addict" or "recovering alcoholic."

I've always been against phrases such as those. They tend to keep you in bondage and make you believe that you are not really free but will always be in a perpetual state of recovery. At drug recovery meetings you are constantly confessing your addiction, which has to be the worst thing to do. "My name is Joe and I am an alcoholic." "My name is Jennifer and I am a recovering heroin addict." "Hi, I'm Bob, and I've been a recovering alcoholic for more than twenty years now." I had been to so many state drug rehab services. None of them worked at all. Sin was the root cause of my problem, and to try and deal with any sin problem without dealing with God is meaningless.

When you continue to confess addictions you literally summon the spirit of that compulsion and in time you will be using drugs or other substances all over again. That concept does not usually have long-lasting effects. And, most drug rehabilitation services controlled by the State have proven to be completely ineffectual, especially since they are not faith-based. After I received salvation, I knew that I was free. I felt brand new and literally felt cleansed. I wholeheartedly connected with this passage:

> *"Therefore, if anyone is in Christ, **he** is a new creation; old things have passed away; behold, all things have become new"* (2 Cor. 5:17, emphasis added).

Most of the people whom I ran around with thought that I was onto a new game, a kind of hustle when they heard that I had received Jesus. Little did they know this was no game. This was no hustle. It was a genuine conversion. To my surprise, shortly after I got saved, I wound up back in jail again, on charges from a previous offense that I committed long before I got saved. Prior to my conversion, the Federal Government could not locate me. But as soon as I received Jesus, they caught me. My friends surely thought that this incarceration would cause me to backslide. But when I went to prison, I actually got closer to God. During that time, the Holy Spirit literally taught me the Word. This was my process. And in that process, I learned how to fast and pray, which, I believe, is the cure for any addictive behavior.

I spent time there from 1976-1978. It was a type of preparation for some of the great things that God would later do in my life. At first I was discouraged. I really believed that God was going to touch the judge's heart and cause him to acquit me. Looking back, I now realize that God was just protecting me and sheltering me from the bad influences that were out there, waiting to destroy me all over again. At the right time and not until, God supernaturally brought me out of jail. How he did it was extraordinary. I was sentenced to serve six years. God caused me to have favor with the parole board, and my sentence was reduced from six years to only two.

I hope that you are getting the point that my entire life has been one miracle after another. I am humbled when I think about where I was and where I am now. God's blessings on my life and His provision are a testament to His faithfulness and merciful compassion. Great Faith Ministries, the church that I pastor, has an active membership of more than 3,000 people, and is one of the fastest growing churches in Detroit. Our broadcast, *Miracles Do Happen,* is televised nationally on various networks reaching millions of homes.

God has prospered our ministry to operate on a multi-million dollar budget. Just to think that once I could not even be trusted with five dollars and now, God has placed the responsibility in my charge to control millions of dollars for His Kingdom. Only God can create such a miracle. Our ministry is filled with countless numbers of miracle conversions like mine. On a regular basis, people are healed of various diseases, from cancer to AIDS to heart disease,

There have been so many occurrences that I have lost count of the number of drug abusers who have been completely delivered by the Lord. Because I went through this horrifying process and came out on top, it helps me to better appreciate the cleansing power of the blood of Jesus that washes away my old man and makes me like Christ. For that reason, I cannot look down on the drug addict, not even for one minute, because I was in their same situation at one time.

What I want you to understand is that, were it not for the miraculous working power of Jesus, I would be dead or, at best, a brain-dead paralyzed vegetable. I am alive because of a miracle. My possessions were miraculously put into my hands. Our church grew as a result of a miraculous outpouring. This book is not just another book; it is a testament of hope. It is a deed, entitling you to all of God's miraculous provisions. God called me out of Egypt, a type of sin, and called me His Son. I am convinced that He will do the same for you.

> *"When he arose, he took the young Child and His mother by night and departed for Egypt, and was there until the death of Herod, that it might be fulfilled which was spoken by the Lord through the prophet, saying, 'Out of Egypt I called My Son'"* (Matt. 2:14-15, emphasis added).

Introduction

As we entered the new millennium I could not help but notice how many people have suddenly taken great interest in the supernatural. Millions of people are being drawn to psychics and fortune tellers to discover their futures and to receive spiritual direction. Scores more are seeking out alternative methods of healing from shamans, believing that they have the power to cleanse the human body from evil spirits, to channeling, where one person becomes a conduit for a deceased person. One of the more modern phenomenons that have surfaced in recent years is the uncanny interest that people have developed in communicating with their deceased relatives and loved ones.

Shows such as *Crossing Over* with John Edwards and *Beyond* with James Van Praagh, both of whom claim that they can communicate with the dead, receive unprecedented ratings by viewers. It has become clear that people now want to experience the supernatural in one way or another. In times past, the supernatural was one of those mysterious phenomenons that most folks intentionally tried to avoid, primarily because they did not understand it at all. They could not explain it, so they did not pursue it. Many other people expressed fear of the unknown and miraculous realms. Their fears led them to totally distance themselves from anything that had to do with miracles or having a spiritual encounter.

However, we have entered a new day, in which a hunger for God is so great that it is literally demanding results. Sadly, this hunger is so great that literally anything will satisfy, truth or falsehood. You may say, "All I can see from my observation of society is wickedness and corruption at best, not a desire for God or the things that relate to God." Surely that is a matter of perception. It has always been interesting to me how two people can see the same situation, yet both interpret it in a totally different way. Where one person's sees misfortune and mayhem, another person may see the misfortune as an opportunity that will bring about good fortune. I see the latter.

Although I do not deny the obvious threats that the enemy has unleashed on our society, there still lies within all of his schemes a much deeper reality. I know that there has been a rise in drug addictions, which translates into increased revenues for drug dealers and higher levels of drug trafficking. It is even difficult to watch the Six O' Clock News and not witness some form of violence, grand theft, child molestation, or rape that has taken place.

If criminal behavior were only a product of street life in urban America it would be one thing. However, any mature thinking person knows well that criminal activity cannot be limited to an urban experience, but is frequently unleashed in cooperate centers within the United States and throughout the world. These actions can be clearly seen in the poor choices that were made that brought about major scandals in Enron, MCI WorldCom, and Tyco Corporations.

What do all of these things mean? Is there a message in all of this? As I previously mentioned, it is all a matter of perception. It simply depends on how you look at things. One train of Christian thought may look at our present condition and immediately want to escape this present darkness. That is a viable option. However, I've decided that sin in the land is only a deeply rooted cry for a Savior who has the ability to deliver them from evil.

Unfortunately, over the years much of Christianity has focused far too much on the sin within our society and not the cure—the Lord Jesus Christ. This improper focus has only led our society into a deeper spiral of doubt, disbelief, and fear. While others seem to feel that the darkness in the world is so great, I say just the opposite—the light within believers is just too dim.

Simply put, the world needs to see our light. They need to see miracles, signs, and wonders. While some may not agree, I believe with all of my heart that miracles will increase as we come near to the close of life as we now perceive it. Beyond any doubt, the world has sent an obvious message to the Church in the form of their lawless conduct, that they desperately need a touch from a miraculous God. Instead of the miracles that they need so desperately, the Church in many instances, has given the world our programs, church policy and practice, the doctrines of men, and a form of godliness, but no power. The result—they are still left wanting.

For those of us who have made the quality decision to demonstrate the miracles of Jesus Christ, we have been criticized without fail. Those criticisms I wear proudly as a badge of honor. Somehow I feel within my spirit that I identify with Jesus more closely when I walk in the miraculous and am criticized for doing so. Jesus healed on the Sabbath, boldly forgave sins, and healed people who were ceremonially unclean. He was never concerned about the status quo. He intentionally tried not to fit into the system of this world. And for that reason He was hated.

He who hates me hates my Father as well. If I had not done among them what no one else did, they would not be guilty of sin. But now they have seen these miracles, and yet they have hated both me and my Father. But this is to fulfill what is written in their Law: "They hated me without reason" (John 15:23-25, NIV).

Although Christ performed these miracles under great scrutiny and judgment from the people, He continued to do the impossible. He never allowed the criticisms of the people to stop Him from accomplishing His mission. Much like the early apostles, I am possessed with an unwavering conviction that God is a God of miracles. Added to that, people who have been filled with the Holy Ghost, evidenced by speaking in tongues and having a spirit of love, are mandated by the Lord Jesus Christ to demonstrate these miracles to unbelievers.

There is an urgent plea for miracles that can no longer be ignored. Can we, as genuinely Spirit-filled believers, continue to allow the enemy to make progress with his counterfeit brand of healing, miracles, signs, and wonders? How long will we ignore the commands of our Lord to heal the sick, cast out devils, and to save the lost? After all, it was Jesus Himself who said,

Go into all the world and preach the gospel to every crea-ture. He who believes and is baptized will be saved; but he who does not believe will be condemned. And these signs will follow those who believe: In My name they will cast out demons; they will speak with new tongues; they will take up serpents; and if they drink anything deadly, it will by no means hurt them; they will lay hands on the sick, and they will recover (Mark 16:15-18).

Are we doing what Jesus commanded, or are we waiting for the right time, when the air has been cleared of naysayers and cynics? While the secular society believes that it has the answers to some of the deepest problems within our world, the Church must rise up and declare the truth of God—"You may have some answers, but we are the answer. Christ in us is the hope of glory." (See Colossians 1:27.)

Please take note of the spiritual forecast. The sound of an abundance of His rain is near. God's power will be greater now than it has ever been before. In this hour you will witness God performing creative miracles such as new kidneys and lungs developing in the body, missing eyeballs and limbs suddenly and mysteriously growing back, and people literally being raised from the dead. While these miracles may not be conventional or common to the mind of the carnal, God desires more than anything to use this manifestation of His power as His ace drawing card.

IT IS MY EARNEST PRAYER THAT NOT ONLY WILL THE WORDS THAT FOLLOW IN THESE CAREFULLY THOUGHT OUT AND SPIRITUALLY PREPARED PAGES GIVE VALIDITY TO MIRACLES, BUT THEY WILL ALSO PROVOKE YOU.

One thing is for sure—when they see the mighty miracles of God they will surely believe on Him—The Lord Jesus Christ. It is my earnest prayer that not only will the words that follow in these carefully thought out and spiritually prepared pages give validity to miracles, but they will also provoke you. I pray that they will provoke you to not only believe that miracles are truly possible and in fact do happen, but that you have been sovereignly chosen by God almighty as His choice vessel through whom these miracles will flow. Accept that challenge. Boldly do the impossible!

"Now while he was in Jerusalem at the Passover Feast, many people saw the miraculous signs he was doing and believed in his name" (John 2:23, NIV).

CHAPTER ONE

Shall Miracles Cease?

For many centuries there have been several renowned theologians and biblical scholars who have taught that the days of miracles are over. Even today, many learned men and women believe and teach that after the original apostles had died, there was no longer a need for miracles, bringing them to an end. Miracles, they taught, were only instituted by God for the purpose of drawing men and women to Him. They were used as a magnetic force to magnify God in the eyes of common man and draw them in through this work of love and matchless power.

Since the Church of the Lord Jesus Christ has been well-established, they teach that miracles are no longer needed. The truth is that miracles were used as a tool to draw unbelievers to Christ in the early church. However, the last time I checked, the world is yet filled with unbelievers. If the truth were told, miracles are needed perhaps more today than any other time in the history of humanity. Not only are they needed, miracles are already very much alive and well.

If you haven't witnessed a miracle lately, then maybe you need to rediscover the God of Scripture. I'll continually repeat that God is a God of miracles. You'll often hear me announce that, *Miracles Do Happen*. Not only is this the name of our broadcast, but this phrase has become my life's creed. More than anything, I know that God cannot be separated from the miracles that He performs any more than wetness can be separated from water. Miracles are the very essence of His goodwill toward mankind. Because God loves us, He gives us miracles as an installment, a type of deposit, to lift us beyond our present circumstances.

GOD CANNOT BE SEPARATED FROM THE MIRACLES THAT HE PERFORMS ANY MORE THAN WETNESS CAN BE SEPARATED FROM WATER.

Those who persist against miracles today are no different than the Pharisaical religious leaders who irritated Jesus with their false accusations, blatant lies, and scandalous remarks. These people are on an assignment from hell to disestablish our divine connection to God, made possible through Jesus Christ. It is Christ's miracles that draw sinners to saving grace. Whether a miracle of love, healing, or financial increase, God uses miracles in one form or another to connect us to Himself.

Since this entire book is all about miracles and getting the Body of Christ ready to receive and give back those miracles we need to have a better foundational understanding of what a miracle actually is. According to the dictionary, *Merriam Webster's Unabridged Dictionary*, a miracle is an action that opposes scientific and natural law. Drawing from that conclusion, a miracle is something that only God can perform. If a miracle is possible for you to perform, then it cannot qualify as a miracle. Only God can work miracles in people's life.

MIR'ACLE

n.

1. an event or action that apparently contradicts known scientific laws and is hence thought to be due to supernatural causes, esp. to an act of God

2. a remarkable event or thing; marvel

3. a wonderful example; a miracle of tact

Merriam-Webster's Unabridged Dictionary version 3.0, copyright 2003.

God performs the miracle through people. With our permission, God uses our bodies as the channels through which miracles flow. But do not be deceived, God and only God works the miracle. God only shows up in the way of the miraculous when all that you have attempted to do in the natural has failed to produce your desired results. For example, a person may have been diagnosed with cancer and the cancer has metastasized throughout their entire body, in which case the chemotherapy has little to no effect...

This person has done all that they know to do in the natural sense. They went to the doctor's, received treatments, and faithfully used the medication prescribed; yet they got worse. This creates a perfect situation for God to work a miracle. If there was anything that the person could do to totally eliminate the cancer themselves, then they would not need God. Added to that, if the person could find a proven remedy to eliminate the cancer, they probably would have used that method already and obtained their healing.

GOD, THROUGH HIS MIRACLE-WORKING POWER, OPPOSES BOTH SCIENTIFIC AND NATURAL LAWS.

You see, God shows up for the impossible cases, the ones we cannot solve or cure. He shows up in cases where everything that you have tried over and over again has miserably failed. God will show up in a dysfunctional marriage relationship that is abusive, manipulative, and nearly a week away from finalizing a divorce. He will enter in and miraculously make that once-torn husband

and wife fall madly in love all over again. God, through His miracle-working power, opposes both scientific and natural laws.

Given this scenario, natural law says that it is better for them to divorce. On the other hand, God's supernatural law says that it is better for them to reconcile. At this very moment, you may be at a point in your life where you've just lost your job yet you have thousands of dollars in bills that you owe. You have no cash-flow. Every week, you have been eagerly searching and filling out numerous applications for employment. Despite your efforts, you still cannot find another job.

Now, all of your savings have become depleted. In this scenario, God is just waiting to oppose scientific and natural law. Natural law says that you will be evicted or foreclosed on. Natural law says that your car will be repossessed and that your credit will begin to rapidly decline. Scientifically speaking, you will probably not be able to pull off earning the thirty or forty thousand dollars that you need literally overnight. So, it appears that you are stuck in a fiscal hole, waiting to die.

Suddenly you receive your miracle. God supernaturally sends a deliverer into your life to show you how to become financially free within thirty days. In thirty days, your net worth goes from a negative dollar amount to more than 3 ½ million dollars. Only a miracle from God could have pulled this off. Others tried to do the same things that you did, yet after thirty days they went into a deeper spiral of debt.

Why is this? It's because God is a God of miracles. And, miracles do happen. You can't force God to do what He does in the same way that He did it before. God never has a rhyme or reason to what He does. If He did things in the same way all the time, you would be more inclined to start focusing on the method and not God. Focusing on the method will inevitably get you deeper into a mess, since methods do and always will change.

34

The whole purpose of this work is to get you to understand the importance of focusing on the Source of all miracles—God. My goal is that you will be encouraged to know that, no matter how dismal and unrealistic your situation may appear to be, you don't have to worry. The very place where God shows up most regularly is in impossible situations. If your situation seems to be an impossible one, get excited. Get excited because you know that God is just around the corner. And there is nothing, absolutely nothing, that He cannot do. Knowing and believing that is the beginning of your miracle.

> *"But Jesus looked at them and said, 'With men it is impossible, but not with God; for with God all things are possible'"* (Mark 10:27).

YOU ARE A MIRACLE

Far too often we try so hard to find a miracle that we wind up overlooking the most obvious one of all—the miracle within us. We look for miracles in everybody other than ourselves. At times, it becomes almost instinctive for us to anticipate hearing a testimony of God's miracle-working power in somebody else, yet not believing that God will do it for you. I've penned this work to let you know that you are a miracle. That's right, you are a miracle. From this moment on, you need to begin making that confession with great conviction. Just say it now, 'I am a miracle.' It may sound strange to you at first, but keep saying it.

THERE IS A SIDE OF YOU THAT IS SO ABSOLUTELY AMAZING, THAT IS DIRECTLY CORRELATED TO THE MIRACULOUS HAND OF GOD WORKING IN YOUR LIFE.

The more you confess it the more it will become real to you. After awhile, you won't be as inclined to search for things in other people that God has already built inside of you. There is greatness

35

on the inside of you that has not even been tapped into yet. There is a side of you that is so absolutely amazing, that is directly correlated to the miraculous hand of God working in your life.

It would probably be a large number if you tried to count just how many people whom you graduated from high school with or whom you went to grade school with who have died a long time ago. Many of your past acquaintances have died, yet have not endured one tenth of the things that you endured. That should make you wonder why you are still alive. Why haven't you died too? You still have the opportunity to make a difference in this life. Yet, you have suffered so many things. There is an element of the miraculous working in your life, which is the very reason that you are still here.

When I speak of *here*, I am not talking about a geographical location such as Detroit, Chicago, Los Angeles, or Milwaukee. When I say *here*, I am speaking of life and the experiences that you will come to treasure as you pursue life. You could very well be a statistic like the people you grew up with in the neighborhood that you lived in. But that did not happen. Our miraculous God totally changed the statistic concerning your future and gave you a totally different report. This change was in and of itself a miracle. Why was it a miracle? The answer is quite simple. You could not have saved yourself, nor did you have the power to turn your own life around. Only God can do that.

Looking at things from that point of view, it becomes easier to accept that miracles cannot die. As long as you are alive, miracles shall not cease, because you are in fact a miracle from God. Your children and your children's children are miracles also. God has made a promise that He cannot take back. He promised to bless your posterity. The fourth and fifth generations that will come after you will need miracles just as you do. Their miracle will begin in the same place that yours began: by accepting the truth of the knowledge that you are one of God's greatest miracles.

THE MIRACLE OF SALVATION—THE NEW BIRTH

Nicodemus said to Him, "How can a man be born when he is old? Can he enter a second time into his mother's womb and be born?" Jesus answered, "Most assuredly, I say to you, unless one is born of water and the Spirit, he cannot enter the kingdom of God. That which is born of the flesh is flesh, and that which is born of the Spirit is spirit. Do not marvel that I said to you, 'You must be born again'" (John 3:4-7).

It has never ceased to amaze me how a person who is steeped in sin can be suddenly made clean and declared righteous by the power of God. How could a person who lived her life as a prostitute be cleansed and viewed by her former clients as a respectable and virtuous woman? Imagine a once big-time gangster and drug dealer transformed by God's saving power, who becomes a deliverer to people who are suffering from drug addictions.

Both the world and, sad to say, the Church, often look at such a man or woman with a critical and condemning eye. They ask, "How can that ex-dealer call himself or herself a child of God? Look at all of the lives they ruined? Ain't no way that God can use them. I wonder if they even know who God is."

Just the opposite, God looks at this same type of person as His opportunity to demonstrate His miraculous power. Of all of the miracles that I have witnessed and have had the humbling privilege of being a small part of, I do not know of any greater miracle than when a person is born again. Although some may think of it as a common act, the new birth can almost be viewed as a phenomenon of sorts. Regardless of how much academic or theological knowledge one has, no one can adequately understand just how someone can really be reborn. It's so amazing!

Even though we cannot explain it adequately with words, the experience is very much a genuine reality in the Kingdom of God.

Nicodemus, a ruler of the Jews, wanted Jesus to explain the miracle of the new birth to him. It was a mystery that continued to rouse his curiosity. He could not understand how a man or woman could physically re-enter their mother's womb as a full-grown adult. That concept did not make any logical sense to him. It became obvious that he had totally missed the point.

He also really wanted to know and understand just how Jesus performed miracles. Deep within, Nicodemus believed that God must have been empowering Jesus to accomplish these wonders, yet he couldn't quite understand how He did them. Nicodemus' colleagues thought that Jesus performed miracles under the influences of demonic power. They thought that He was some kind of warlock, performing incantations and casting spells. Their spiritual ignorance blinded them to the knowledge of God's miracle-working power in the same way that spiritual ignorance blinds people today.

Jesus proceeded to tell Nicodemus that it would be a waste of time to even try to explain how He performed the miracles until he was first born again. Only those who have been born again have a fair chance at understanding the mysteries of the Kingdom. The mystery is that we are born of the Spirit of God. In other words, we take on the nature of God through this new birth process. And as a result, we are able to communicate with God and understand His supernatural workings.

Nicodemus childishly believed that he would have to re-enter his mother's womb, wait for nine months, and be delivered again by a midwife in order to experience his new birth. Jesus immediately interrupted his thought pattern by explaining that, in order to experience the miracle of the new birth, one must be born of the water and of the spirit. Some scholars have interpreted being born of the water as being born of the water that exists inside of the amniotic sac inside a woman's uterus. This interpretation qualifies only humans who are created by the hands of God as being capable of receiving salvation, which does not include human clones.

Another thought about being born of the water centers on water baptism as a symbol and testimony of one's committed faith in Jesus. This water baptism experience mirrors the death, burial, and resurrection of Jesus. For that reason, all believers are expected to willingly receive water baptism as a sign of their salvation and identification with our Lord's suffering.

Then there is the Spirit. The new birth requires that you be born of the Spirit. This element is what perpetuates the miraculous. Only the Spirit of God can change a person from a sinner to a saint. Only God can instantaneously take away the desire to use drugs, even though a person may have been addicted for more than a decade. Only by God's Spirit can a person who was wholeheartedly committed to the Taliban, a Moslem fundamentalist terrorist group, be instantly converted to a relationship with Christ and become one of the greatest evangelists known to mankind.

An example of this is Reza Safa, who was born and reared in a Muslim family in the Middle East. He became a practicing and devout Shiite Muslim. He faithfully practiced the rules and regulations of the faith. He would always be sure to fast during the month of Ramadan and pray five times each day. After he graduated from high school, Reza left the Middle East in search of a more fulfilling future. It was then that he heard the gospel message for the very first time and received Jesus.

Today he conducts crusades all around the world, having traveled to more than forty countries, proclaiming the name of Jesus. You can read more about his the story of his conversion and how to reach out to Muslim people in his book entitled, *Inside Islam: Exposing and Reaching the World of Islam,* Charisma House Publishers. If anything, Reza should have become an even more devout Muslim as he grew older, defending his faith at any cost. But God interrupted his life and called him into full time Christian ministry. This is nothing short of a miracle.

These all are miracles of great proportions. From street hustlers to Wall Street investors, from convicted felons to Supreme Court Judges, from petty thieves to Presidents of Humanitarian organizations, from illiterates to PhD's, from murderers to life-giving medical doctors, the new birth supernaturally changes once-hopeless sinners into hope-filled achievers. Life itself would have given up on most people who fit into the negative profiles of the past.

But the miracle of the new birth looks not at what you were, but rather at what you are capable of becoming. It's like getting a clean slate. God gives people a fresh start. Everything in the past has been cleared off of your record and now you get to start from the present. That alone is reason enough for every person to ask God to give him or her the greatest miracle of the "new birth."

> *Therefore, if anyone is in Christ, **he is** a new creation; old things have passed away; behold, all things have become new* (2 Cor. 5:17, emphasis added).

BEWARE OF THE MODERN-DAY PHARISEE— AN ENEMY TO YOUR MIRACLE

One of the greatest enemies to your miracle is a modern-day Pharisee. Before you draw a simple conclusion, don't be deceived into believing that a Pharisee is an unlearned person. Pharisees are not ignorant of biblical tradition. They are rather well-versed in the Scriptures, so much so that they become bored with the law and decide to add to it.

Most Pharisees were scholars of the law and understood rabbinical teachings well. They did not lack the knowledge of God's Word. Believe it or not, they really did not lack wisdom in being able to execute the Word of God in many cases. Where most Pharisees lacked was in the area of receiving the revelation of Jesus Christ for their own lives. They neither understood nor did they accept the power of Christ.

They would receive clear signs from heaven concerning the reality of Jesus Christ as Messiah, particularly through the miracles that Jesus performed regularly. Despite how conspicuous the miracle was, most Pharisees would not only deny the work of the miracle, but also falsely attribute the work of God as being a work of the devil. They did not realize that this was a very dangerous thing to do. They would begin to falsely accuse Jesus of being a fraud, a criminal, and an imposter.

The reason why they were so against Jesus is because the things that Jesus did now and then openly opposed their traditions. It went against what was accepted as normal. For most Pharisees, there was nothing more valuable to them than their traditions. They worshipped their traditions. So, they looked at Jesus as an enemy to their tradition. In all actuality, Jesus was not intending to destroy tradition, but rather, to redefine the whole concept. There are some traditions that have proven to be favorable. Then there are many other traditions that totally oppose God's Word. Jesus came to make a clear distinction between the two.

The Pharisees hated Jesus for attempting to bring such light to an ignorant people. They wanted things to remain the way that they always had been. They wanted their traditions to stay the way they always were. But the problem became very intense, because most of their man-made traditions were diametrically opposed to the Word of God. And wherever their traditions were upheld, the Word of God became totally ineffective. It just would not work.

> *He said to them, "All too well you reject the command-ment of God, that you may keep your tradition [...] mak-ing the word of God of no effect through your tradition which you have handed down. And many such things you do"* (Mark 7:9,13).

Jesus knew that, wherever these traditions were supported, God's Word would have no power there and hence, miracles could not flow freely. Whenever Jesus could not perform miracles in the Bible, it was directly connected to the spirit of the people in that region, who refused to give up their limiting traditions. One example of this is when Jesus could not perform any miracles in His own country because everyone there knew who He was and because of that they became all too familiar with Him, causing them not to believe in His power.

"And he did not many mighty works there because of their unbelief." (Matt. 13:58, KJV).

That's why Jesus is still looking for people today who will openly oppose traditions that conflict with God's Word. Remember that just because something is your tradition does not make it right.

But woe to you, scribes and Pharisees, hypocrites! For you shut up the kingdom of heaven against men; for you neither go in yourselves, nor do you allow those who are entering to go in. Woe to you, scribes and Pharisees, hypocrites! For you devour widows' houses, and for a pretense make long prayers. Therefore you will receive greater condemnation. Woe to you, scribes and Pharisees, hypocrites! For you travel land and sea to win one proselyte, and when he is won, you make him twice as much a son of hell as yourselves (Matt. 23:13-15).

This is a detailed depiction of exactly how God felt about the scribes and Pharisees. He begins with a straightforward manner, calling them hypocrites. They pretended to be lovers of God and His people, but were rather lovers of their traditions and selves. God's Kingdom is closed off to anyone who practices and is bound by their traditions.

You may not have been around an ancient Pharisee in person, but I am pretty sure that you may have seen the modern-day

Pharisee, who makes long prayers in order to be seen by men. They want people to believe that they are spiritual and holy. They can quote all of the scriptures, yet they have no love for God's people.

It does not matter to them whether you receive your healing or not. If you die prematurely it does not really matter to them. The Pharisee of today and yesterday both think alike. They are against your miracle, against your freedom, and against the life that God intends for you to enjoy. You must beware of their erroneous spirit, whose intent is to kill, steal, and destroy, just like satan.

ARE HERESY HUNTERS SCRIPTURAL?

Today, there are a number of groups that receive a tremendous amount of church-supported giving, whose primary function is to scrutinize ministries to determine whether or not they are scriptural and valid ministries, based on their opinions. They make conclusive decisions based on their probing on whether they believe a church, a minister, or a para-church ministry actually qualifies to receive their personal approval. These groups are often called heresy hunters and are often labeled as watchdog groups. They have offices, loyal supporters, a mission statement, and operate in a way that appears to be ministry-oriented.

Although these groups seem to have a following, it is, to some extent, ambiguous to me exactly why they exist. They believe that God has called them to caution people everywhere about who is authentically saved from whom they believe are charlatans. They profess to be biblically-based ministries who have created a job to bring all churches and ministries to their level of financial accountability. For example, if a targeted church or ministry does not comply with the watchdog's self imposed standards, then they become labeled as a suspect church or ministry.

That may be a bit difficult to believe at first, but it's really true. It's as if someone that you do not know and you are not in any kind of relationship with suddenly comes up to you and begins asking you for all of your financial statements (bank statements, investments, real estates and other real assets, intellectual property, stocks and bonds, mutual funds, 401K's, IRA's), and asks how you run your financial life, and you obviously refuse to give them answers.

According to most watchdog groups, you would be in total violation of God's Word and will. You wouldn't be in violation because you committed a sinful act. It would simply be because they have claimed to have a word from God concerning financial accountability, so they expect you to automatically believe and surrender all of your privileged information to them because of their claims.

If you choose not to, then they actually post your church and name on the internet web sites and, in mass-printed material, express to the general public that you should not be trusted because you refused to surrender church and ministry financial information to total strangers or even worse, to enemies of your ministry. Feeble-minded Christians and non-believers begin to falsely and unfairly make judgments against the ministry based on "watchdog ministry" reports.

These ministries do not only probe in the area of finances, but they also probe equally as much if not more in the area of miracles. On specific assignments, ministry officials will travel around the country and will often pose as people who are sincerely seeking a touch from the Lord in the area of healing. They will fake, as if they need a healing miracle from God, intentionally trying to expose some level of falsehood in the person and people who are teaming together to conduct the crusade.

These so-called crusaders of righteousness will stand outside of a miracle crusade and hold large picket signs trying to persuade people to avoid going inside, where they'll be brainwashed with the false message that God is a God of miracles. They do this with heartfelt good intentions. They believe with all of their hearts that miracles no longer happen and that whoever preaches that they still exist is a false prophet who is preaching another gospel. They are sincere, but sincerely wrong.

The only reason they follow ministers from town to town and investigate miracles is to accuse them. They believe that accusing is a scriptural ministry, and it rightfully is. However, it is not a ministry of the Lord Jesus Christ. It is a biblical ministry of the devil himself. God, in His Word, clearly depicts satan and nicknames him the accuser—the one who brings charges against God's people. John the Revelator made this point crystal-clear in God's revelation to him.

> *Then I heard a loud voice saying in heaven, "Now salvation, and strength, and the kingdom of our God, and the power of His Christ have come, for the accuser of our brethren, who accused them before our God day and night, has been cast down* (Rev. 12:10).

In this scripture, the accuser of our brethren is cast down. The word brethren in the Old Testament meant one who is kin by birth, and is from the same parents. In the New Testament, the concept of brethren has become expanded to mean anyone who has experienced the new birth, whose Father is the Lord. This person has become a part of the much larger universal brotherhood and sisterhood of man. There are striking similarities between heresy hunters and accusers of the brethren. Both groups bring accusations against God's people every day and every night.

JESUS' ENCOUNTERS WITH HERESY HUNTERS

Jesus encountered this accusatory spirit on various occasions. He most commonly dealt with this accusing spirit whenever

45

He was going to perform a miraculous act by healing someone that the doctors could not. The heresy hunters or watchdogs of today behave the same as the false accusers of Jesus. They watched Jesus closely, not to receive His blessing, but rather to accuse the Lord. They waited patiently to find an area where they believed, by their own interpretations, that Jesus' actions violated Jewish law. As soon as they found what they considered to be concrete reasoning, they came against the Lord like a ton of bricks. The text:

> *Now it happened on another Sabbath, also, that He entered the synagogue and taught. And a man was there whose right hand was withered. So the scribes and Pharisees **watched Him** closely, whether He would heal on the Sabbath, that they might find an **accusation** against Him. But He knew their thoughts, and said to the man who had the withered hand, "Arise and stand here." And he arose and stood. Then Jesus said to them, "I will ask you one thing: Is it lawful on the Sabbath to do good or to do evil, to save life or to destroy?" And when He had looked around at them all, He said to the man, "Stretch out your hand." And he did so, and his hand was restored as whole as the other. But **they were filled with rage,** and discussed with one another what they might do to Jesus (Luke 6:6-11, emphasis added).*

Even though this man who had suffered with a withered hand was miraculously healed by the power of God, the heresy hunters where **filled with rage.** Why were they so angry and hateful? Jesus did not do anything wrong. You would think that they would be exhilarated and overjoyed since this man had been released from a long-time malady. But being glad is not their purpose. Their purpose is to totally destroy the anointing and power of God. These people in modern times parade as messengers of light but deny the power of God. They speak of Jesus to make people believe that they know Him, yet they persecute the saints of the Lord rather than win souls to Christ.

It may seem as if they are winning souls to the Lord by their numbers and overall support, but they are only aggressively recruiting and training a highly skilled army of assassins, called accusers. They will stop at nothing. They won't cease until you and your influence has long died. Jesus healed the sick, raised the dead, cast out demons, and performed various miracles. Yet, the heresy hunters crucified him and, while he was dying, they held over His head an accusation that, although they thought it was untrue, had far more relevance than they could ever know.

> *"Now it was the third hour, and they crucified Him. And the inscription of His accusation was written above: THE KING OF THE JEWS"* (Mark 15:25-26, emphasis added).

There is no such Kingdom ministry as a heresy hunter or a watchdog ministry. Those are ministries of satan. Any biblically-based ministry that represents the kingdom of God does not have time to judge another man's or woman's ministry. True Kingdom ministry is so occupied with winning and recruiting souls for the glory of God that they really are not aware of who is doing what. If anyone needs to be judged it's our self. We should be more concerned about whether or not our own lifestyles and the service that we give are pleasing to God, rather than dwell on the validity of our brother's or sister's ministry.

Just like Jesus' accusers judged Him falsely because they did not understand what He was doing, ministries of satan have set up shop to do the same things today. They had never seen the miracles performed in such a manner. Since they had never seen it before, they immediately cast it off as being heresy. That is an extreme case of spiritual bigotry. To believe that what you know or the revelation of God that you think you have outweighs what God is doing here and now is arrogance and bigotry at its best.

If conventional Christians have not seen God move in a certain way, most of them cancel it off as not being from God. Or even worse, they become extremely judgmental of everything they see. It's a very dangerous thing to try to judge God's power in someone. God's power will never be limited by our restrictive and petty judgment. He's much bigger than that, and we should be too.

> *Judge not, and you shall not be judged. Condemn not, and you shall not be condemned. Forgive, and you will be forgiven* (Luke 6:37).

OVER? WE'VE ONLY JUST BEGUN

So how long will miracles last? The answer is plain and simple—until Jesus returns. Until He comes again, expect your miracle. Despite what people say that is negative, miracles are here to stay. In a world where violence runs rampant and wars and the rumors of war increase each minute, we need to be in constant view of God's miracles.

In fact, if we as believers do not live in a constant mode of expectancy, we may miss the miracle of Christ's return. The Bible makes it clear that even the return of the Lord will be in a very miraculous manner. The way that He will return will defy the laws of gravity and of nature. "Then they will see the Son of Man **coming in a cloud** with power and great glory. Now when these things begin to happen, look up and lift up your heads, because your redemption draws near" (Luke 21:27-28, NKJV, emphasis added). Jesus will return in a miraculous way, in a cloud.

> *For the Lord Himself will descend from heaven with a shout, with the voice of an archangel, and with the trumpet of God. And the dead in Christ will rise first. Then we who are alive **and** remain shall be caught up together with them in the clouds to meet the Lord in the air. And thus we shall always be with the Lord. Therefore comfort one another with these words* (1 Thess. 4:16-18, emphasis added).

The very nature of the rapture or the catching away of the saints is miraculous. The Bible declares that dead people will rise up and be caught up to meet Christ in the air. According to the laws of gravity and of death and life this cannot be possible. Only a miraculous God can cause the dead to be resurrected and then give them the ability to begin their heavenly pursuit. The very idea of a resurrection is miraculous in every way.

I believe that God desires that we now get comfortable and accustomed to the miraculous. He wants us to be accustomed to seeing the dead raised, believing that people empowered by God can literally walk on water, and that those who are terminally ill will be completely healed by Christ's power. It is this atmosphere of expectancy that will accommodate and welcome the Lord when He returns to meet His Bride. Expect miracles to become a reality in your life. They are here to stay!

CHAPTER TWO

Birthed Out of Crisis

One of the things that I want you to realize is that a miracle is birthed out of crisis. Now there are some preachers that teach against miracles for this very reason. They believe that since miracles are the answer to a crisis that we should rather seek to live under the divine blessings and favor of God rather than to look for a miracle that will deliver us from our crisis. Although this train of thought may seem acceptable, let's look at this whole area of crisis a little deeper.

The word crisis means a time of great danger or trouble. The end of a crisis is frequently unpleasant. Another meaning of the word crisis is a turning point in the course of anything. It is a decisive or crucial time in a person's life or in their health. It can have both positive and negative implications. We've heard terms used in the United States of America such as we are in an "economic crisis."

When we hear statements such as these it lets us know two very important things. The first thing we learn is that there has been a turning point in the economy. The economy changed either from good to bad or bad to worse. The second thing that is very important to recognize is that unless there were a high standard upheld in the economy no one would really know how to measure whether the economy had gone bad or not.

For example, there are some countries such as Haiti in which the crisis that they are experiencing has become so commonplace for them that a bad economy and widespread poverty have become normal to them. Their crisis is a general characteristic of the country. In other words, if someone mentions the country of Haiti here in America, one of the very first things that comes to mind, particularly for the believer, is that Haiti is a mission field that needs much financial support and prayer because they are impoverished.

In some ways, we have come to accept their crisis as being such a familiar place that to be any other way would be totally abnormal. What's my point? My point is that people today have come to accept your crisis as being normal also. Only you can change their perception. No one is immune to a crisis. However, there are two types of crises for people, countries, families, and marriages. Your type of crisis will determine the kind of miracle needed to deliver you from your crisis. The first type is the crisis that you have not come to accept as being normal since you were not born into it.

Perhaps an outside force provoked your situation to begin to decline. You can distinctly remember when things were not as awful as they are now. You remember so well how things used to be. And because you have that vision to hold onto, you live your life everyday with great expectation that one day the hope of our salvation, Jesus Christ Himself, will recognize your condition and rescue you from it. This scenario can be best understood by looking at the life of someone who has gone from riches to rags. They were rich before, so their richness is a point of reference for them.

This is much like the first generation of slaves who came to America from Africa, who had tasted what freedom was actually like. They clearly remembered being rulers over regions and provinces. They remembered the lifestyle that they once enjoyed. Strong families were a central part of African culture. To be torn away from their heritage, their family, and the economic base was an abnormal situation for them. They refused to become accustomed to their new crisis.

The second type of crisis is the one that I began to deal with. This type of crisis has no reference point. It has never seen wealth or good health. This kind does not understand what it means to have a strong family life. This crisis does not even know how to define needs particularly from the perspective that most people in the United States of America define needs.

We define needs differently than people who live life experiencing the second kind of crisis. In America, we are taught that we need a car, a home, and fine clothes to wear. I can see the relevance of these claims in light of our society's expectations and the ever-changing trends. However, people in impoverished countries of the world have never owned a home or even seen a fancy car, and they wear rags. For these, needs are defined totally differently.

Their needs are having suitable drinking water to replace the contaminated poisonous water that runs through their villages. They desire to have at least one meal each day, rather than having to wait a week at a time just to eat dinner. They don't seem to mind running around half naked—just give them a clean river to bathe in and they will be fine. They don't need our paper money. They just want to have soil rich in nutrients that can produce high-quality fruit and vegetables that they can use for their food and for trading. Their needs are completely different than ours.

What you need to understand is that both the first and second crisis both qualifies as crisis. And every human will in his or her lifetime experience one of these crises if they have not already. I've already acknowledged that great preachers and teachers have taught that we should rather live under the divine favor of God and not look to have a miracle all of the time. I agree wholeheartedly.

My only concern is that I am not sure that it is possible in a sin-infested society that demands miracles. People in sin and those affected by its deadly poison will always stand in need of a miracle. God's Kingdom is truly supposed to be established on this earth just like it is in heaven. However, with the amount of separation, segregation, and other divisions that exist in the Body of Christ, I am not sure that we are very close to accomplishing that goal. When that goal of unity in the Body has been accomplished, then we will never have to guard against a crisis. But until that time comes, crisis will be a natural part of life.

Those who do not agree have either never experienced a crisis or are denying that they have ever experienced a crisis. Either position will eventually prove to be totally unfruitful. It is this type of thinking that makes people believe that their physical strength and human reasoning are what gets things accomplished in the spirit world. It is not about how strong you are. If you were really all that strong you wouldn't be in the situation that you are in now. It is only in resting in God's strength where we will ultimately find our answer, our strength for the journey, and of course, our miracle. Paul made it plain when he wrote:

> *And He said to me, "My grace is sufficient for you, for My strength is made perfect in weakness." Therefore most gladly I will rather boast in my infirmities, that the power of Christ may rest upon me. Therefore I take pleasure in infirmities, in reproaches, in needs, in persecutions, in distresses, for Christ's sake. For when I am weak, then I am strong* (2 Cor. 12:9-10).

All throughout the Bible this pattern of miracles being birthed out of a crisis is very clear. The majority of people that Jesus healed were in the midst of a major crisis. Their faith in the time of crisis is what attracted Jesus to them. Does this mean that I am glorifying and embellishing crises? Absolutely not! I do not like to experience crisis any more than you do. What I am trying to do is to reach out to you if you are going through the middle of a crisis.

Maybe your crisis has just begun. I want you to know more than anything that your miracle is lying right in the center of your crisis. It's not very far away. No matter what you are dealing with, God is a God of miracles. He has already made a way for you to escape the deadly effects of your crisis. You shall live and not die. You shall prosper beyond your imagination and live long to proclaim the goodness of the Lord.

A WIDOWED WOMAN IN CRISIS

*"Arise, go to Zarephath, which **belongs** to Sidon, and dwell there. See, I have commanded a widow there to provide for you." So he arose and went to Zarephath. And when he came to the gate of the city, indeed a widow was there gathering sticks. And he called to her and said, "Please bring me a little water in a cup, that I may drink." And as she was going to get it, he called to her and said, "Please bring me a morsel of bread in your hand." So she said, "As the Lord your God lives, I do not have bread, only a handful of flour in a bin, and a little oil in a jar; and see, I am gathering a couple of sticks that I may go in and prepare it for myself and my son, that we may eat it, and die"* (1 Kings 17:9-12, emphasis added).

There is something that you must know. *Your crisis is the very thing that will attract your miracle.* In the same way that bees are naturally attracted to honey, God is supernaturally attracted to your crisis. In the above text we find a woman whose husband has previously died, leaving her without enough money to live on. Added to her destitution, this woman finds herself in the middle of a great famine in her country. If those things represented her only problems, it would be bad enough.

This widow woman also had to face the reality of the fact that her son was lying at the point of death, and there was nothing that she could do to reverse that. Most people then and now would look upon this woman with great despair and feel sorrow for her condition. That is not how God looks at such situations. God saw that this woman was in the middle of a very real crisis. She had no money, no food, and a dying child, with no one to help her. Yet God did not feel sorry for her.

LIKE A MAGNET, GOD IS PULLED TOWARD THE VERY CENTER OF OUR CIRCUMSTANCE IF OUR HEARTS AND MINDS ARE IN OBEDIENCE TO HIS WORD.

God instead became excited for her. He realized that, in a short amount of time, this woman's life would be totally turned right side up. All of those things that we tend to pity are attractive items to God. Like a magnet, God is pulled toward the very center of our circumstance if our hearts and minds are in obedience to His Word. In order for this woman to be delivered from her apparent crisis, she had to exercise faith. Faith is that intangible force that pulls your miracle out of God's bosom and places it safely within yours.

The prophet Elijah had just left a brook called Cherith, which literally means separation. Its meaning is significant because you must separate yourself from anything that has the potential to come against your miracle. Anything that will prevent you from receiving your miracle should be cut off. It could be family members, friends, or present or past successes.

Remember that the enemy of your next miracle is always your last miracle. The prophet Elijah had received miracles from God at the brook at Cherith. Now it was time for him to move to the place of his next miracle. A better way of looking at it is that Elijah was moving from the place where he received his miracle to the place where he would become someone's miracle.

Becoming the miracle that another person only dreamed of is always the higher position. Being a blessing is greater than receiving a blessing. God told Elijah to go to Zarephath and a widow woman would sustain him. Right off the bat, it appeared that Elijah was going to lose, especially if you look at the situations through man's eyes. Why would God send him to a place to be taken care of by a widow woman who does not have enough food or money to sustain herself?

When Elijah came near to the place, this woman was gathering sticks so she could make a fire and prepare her last meal. One of the things that is very interesting to note about this woman is that she was not some charity case waiting for any favors. She knew that she was in a desperate situation, yet the prophet first discovers her doing something. She was participating in her miracle. God wants you to be actively involved in your miracle too.

As I've already established, there are some things that only God can do. Don't even think about trying to do His work. You are guaranteed to fail. However, there are things that you can do to demonstrate that you are operating in faith. For this woman, her demonstrative act was as simple as gathering sticks. That for her was an act of faith. She knew quite well and even confessed to the prophet that she would prepare her last meal and then anticipate the death of her son and herself.

Just think about it for a minute. If you had only one more meal to eat before you died, would you be overly exited about preparing that meal? How could you really enjoy the food, knowing that you're going to die soon after? I believe that this woman, deep down within, prayed that God would deliver her out of her crisis. As a comfort to buy the time between now and the manifestation of her miracle, she chose to be occupied.

In one sense, this woman seemed to be busy doing something that would eventually produce what she desired. She was preparing a meal for her son and herself. Whether she had plenty of cornmeal and oil or little, she would go about preparing her meal in the same manner. The point that I am trying to convey is that you have to learn how to continue to do things as usual until your miracle arrives. Since faith is an action word you have to continue to stand in faith until your miracle manifests.

YOU HAVE TO LEARN HOW TO CONTINUE TO DO THINGS AS USUAL UNTIL YOUR MIRACLE ARRIVES.

You cannot afford to let the enemy see you exposing your fears and inner-inhibitions. Many of the older saints used to say, "Don't let the enemy see you sweat." I totally agree with them. When the enemy senses nervousness in you, he will kill you. In the same way that a snake charms its prey, subduing it through fear and then attacking for the kill, the enemy desires to do the same to you. If you are consistent and busy doing what you regularly do, the enemy won't have time to subdue you.

He will immediately try to find someone who is a far easier target than you are, one who will give him the least resistance when he attacks. So in spite of her crisis, she continued to work. She did not let everything go. She did not drop it all. She was gathering sticks. What about you? In the midst of your crisis will God find you doing something or will He will find you complaining about your pending troubles? Faith is action. And God is always looking for someone who is willing to act on what they believe.

GOD IS ALWAYS LOOKING FOR SOMEONE WHO IS WILLING TO ACT ON WHAT THEY BELIEVE.

Little did this woman realize that she was already in her faith process even before the man of God asked her to make him a cake. Although she did not quite see her deliverance at first, she did not give the prophet great resistance to his request because she had been in the practice of exercising her faith. The scripture explains that this woman did exactly what the man of God asked her to do.

As a result, God blessed her supernaturally. Prophet Elijah was her packaged miracle. Now she was the community's packaged miracle. Because she obeyed God by getting involved with her miracle process, she had so much oil and meal that she could help to sustain her family and neighbors until the famine ended. Her son, who was sick to the point of death later died but was resurrected by God through Elijah. This widowed woman's crisis attracted her miracle.

"So she went away and did according to the word of Elijah; and she and he and her household ate for many days. The bin of flour was not used up, nor did the jar of oil run dry, according to the word of the Lord which He spoke by Elijah" (1 Kings 17:15-16).

A PARENT AND CHILD CRISIS

*While He was still speaking, **some** came from the ruler of the synagogue's **house** who said, "Your daughter is dead. Why trouble the Teacher any further?" As soon as Jesus heard the word that was spoken, He said to the ruler of the synagogue, "Do not be afraid; only believe." And He permitted no one to follow Him except Peter, James, and John the brother of James. Then He came to the house of the ruler of the synagogue, and saw a tumult and those who wept and wailed loudly. When He came in, He said to them, "Why make this commotion and weep? The child is not dead, but sleeping." And they ridiculed Him. But when He had put them all outside, He took the father and the mother of the child, and those **who were** with Him, and entered where the child was lying. Then He took the child by the hand, and said to her, "Talitha, cumi," which is translated, "Little girl, I say to you, arise." Immediately the girl arose and walked, for*

*she was twelve years of age. And they were overcome with
great amazement* (Mark 5:35-42, emphasis added).

If you were a parent, how would you feel if you suddenly
received news that your child had died? Your first reaction to the
news would probably cause you to be in total denial. You would
get squeamish feelings and probably go into a total state of
shock. Then the aftershock would leave you feeling totally devas-
tated and at a lost. I'm sure that is the same way that this ruler
must have felt when he received this alarming news about his
twelve-year-old daughter.

The news that came from messengers about this ruler's
daughter dying officially announced his crisis. Your crisis may be
an official notice sent to you by certified mail. Someone may call
you by telephone to officially announce your crisis. You may
receive an e-mail that declares that your crisis has already begun.
No matter how it comes you will know for sure that it has
arrived. And when it comes it never feels good. It was apparent
that this ruler needed a miracle in the midst of his crisis.

In those days there were professional mourners who were
hired to mourn and cry over a person who had died. They would
do this from the point of death until several days after the burial.
There were people in the house who already began to weep and
wail loudly. Their wailing symbolized sorrow and grief because of
the finality of this young child's life—the end of her destiny. How
can you reverse a death after the physician has declared a child as
dead? You cannot, only Christ the Greatest Physician can change
such a decision by working a miracle.

BUT WHEN IT COMES TO JESUS, THAT WHICH IS CON-
SIDERED NORMAL IS ALWAYS CHALLENGED.

As strange as it may sound, this young girl's death was the
breeding ground that birthed a miracle. Things can't get much

worse than being dead. For the most part, after a person has died, no one would even expect them to come alive again. But when it comes to Jesus, that which is considered normal is always challenged. Things that are average are always confronted by the supernatural.

Jesus said two very strange things to this man. The first thing that Jesus said was, "Do not be afraid; only believe." Before He even raised this child from the dead, Jesus was giving this man a secret message. He let him know in advance that his faith in Him would produce a miracle beyond his imagination. I believe that Jesus is saying the same thing to you today. "Do not be afraid; only believe."

Maybe the doctor has given you a prognosis that is negative. "Do not be afraid; only believe." Perhaps your teenage child was just arrested on drug trafficking charges and has been sentenced to thirty years in prison. "Do not be afraid; only believe." Your husband may have just walked out on you and your children, leaving you to rear them all by yourself. "Do not be afraid; only believe."

Right now you may feel that you are at your lowest point in your life, and you feel like giving up. "Do not be afraid; only believe." All of your money has been spent and you don't have enough to pay any of your bills or buy food for your children. Now you just don't know what to do. Jesus is speaking prophetically to everyone of you, "Do not be afraid; only believe. If you will just believe, I will turn things around for you."

The second important thing that Jesus said was, "The child is not dead, but sleeping." This child was obviously dead. The child had stopped breathing. It has always been interesting to me that Jesus never sees things quite the way we do. What we see as dead, Christ sees in a holding pattern. That's what Jesus wants you to know. The things that were dear to you that you thought were dead are really not dead; they are just in a holding pattern.

Your ministry is not dead. Your family is not dead. You have not lost your influence just yet. Although it may seem as if it has been a while, God still wants to use you. More than anything, He wants you to experience His blessing. But first, you have to recognize that God has not thrown you away. He has not forgotten about you. YOU ARE NOT DEAD! You are only in a holding pattern. Think of it like this, you are waiting patiently in line.

YOU HAVE TO RECOGNIZE THAT GOD HAS NOT THROWN YOU AWAY. HE HAS NOT FORGOTTEN ABOUT YOU. YOU ARE NOT DEAD!

This man who had thought that the enjoyment that he shared with his daughter was over began to shift his beliefs. This man and his wife showed Jesus where the daughter was, they began to trust the Lord and began to envision their daughter alive and well. Jesus told the little girl to arise out of her crisis and she arose. What attracted Jesus to this unassuming family? Was it their noble status or was it their affinity for Hebrew tradition? Hopefully, it is becoming clearer to you that Jesus is attracted to your crisis. For it is in this place where the miracle working power of God manifests itself. ARISE!

A NATION IN CRISIS

And the Lord said to Moses, "When you go back to Egypt, see that you do all those wonders before Pharaoh which I have put in your hand. But I will harden his heart, so that he will not let the people go. Then you shall say to Pharaoh, 'Thus says the Lord: Israel is My son, My firstborn. So I say to you, let My son go that he may serve Me. But if you refuse to let him go, indeed I will kill your son, your first-born'" (Exod. 4:21-23).

For more than six thousand years the nation of Israel has been the center of a major crisis. While modern-day political figures may view Israel's struggle as a factional issue, it is far greater than that. The problem within the tiny state of Israel has been an ongoing problem ever since God declared His affinity for this people. Enslaved under the fascist rulership of Pharaoh, the children of Israel experienced unusually negative treatment from the Egyptians who continually failed to recognize who these people were.

An area of great confusion is when people do not know who you are. When people don't realize your true value they become forced to treat you like a slave. This happened with the children of Israel under the hand of Pharaoh. This abusiveness perpetuated its cycle during the Jewish Holocaust, where Hitler systematically killed off more than six million European Jews by the Nazis, prior to and during World War II.

Because European colonizers failed to recognize the worth and value of Native American Indians, they were killed, tortured, and robbed of their land and property. Africans were sold into slavery and brought to the United States of America to help build this country's economic strength through forced labor, because many white Americans then did not understand their value. When you fail to understand the true worth of a person a crisis will inevitably emerge out of that misunderstanding.

WHEN YOU FAIL TO UNDERSTAND THE TRUE WORTH OF A PERSON A CRISIS WILL INEVITABLY EMERGE OUT OF THAT MISUNDERSTANDING.

It does not matter if it is an individual, a wife who fails to understand her husband's worth, a husband who continually discounts his wife, or parents who refuse to properly value their children. Regardless of how you look at it, abusiveness and destruction are bound to happen where worth is not perceived. This is what happened with the children of Israel, God's people of promise. Their crisis and abuse literally attracted the power and provision of God. Not only will God deliver you from your critical situation, but He will also take good care of you while you are in it.

Added to that, God Himself will fight for you when the enemy comes against you. If your adversary refuses to release what rightfully belongs to you, then God will remove it from the enemy's hands for you. There are some people who, like Pharaoh, have hardened their hearts against God, His Word, and His people. They have become calloused in their reasoning and determined to persecute and torture the people of God.

This is not just a situation that happened in Egypt, but it happens still today. At times, it seems like it will take a miracle to soften the hearts of some people. It's true. Some people will never change unless God causes them to. Don't fret about it. God is in the business of changing seemingly impossible hearts and freeing people from bondage.

You would be amazed to find out how people within your circles, or people who attend church with you have gone through unbelievable predicaments in their lifetime. Yet to look at them you don't see any sign of them having gone through anything at all. Miraculously, God preserved them from the appearance of having been beaten and mistreated by the enemy.

Although they suffered some of the worst treatment, God has allowed them to enter into their wealthy places without any visible signs of having gone through a wilderness experience. God promised to prosper an entire nation, and He delivered on that promise. God is concerned about you; He is also concerned for the nations. His loving care transcends all races and genders. And God will stop at nothing to prove His care for you, even at the cost of a miracle. As with Israel, God promises that, when you have gone through your trials and tribulations, you will enter your place of wealth and prominence. Withstanding your crisis will reward you with abundance.

"Thou hast caused men to ride over our heads; we went through fire and through water: but thou broughtest us out into a wealthy place" (Ps. 66:12, KJV).

JESUS, OUR LORD WAS LITERALLY BIRTHED IN CRISIS

"Nevertheless death reigned from Adam to Moses, even over those who had not sinned according to the likeness of the transgression of Adam, who is a type of Him who was to come" (Rom. 5:14).

"And she will bring forth a Son, and you shall call His name Jesus, for He will save His people from their sins" (Matt. 1:21).

A final yet worthwhile thought concerning this matter is that Jesus was birthed by and into a crisis. He was born to die the death of a criminal. Although he committed no wrong, He would have to bear the sins of the entire world upon himself. There were many facets of our Lord's crisis. Matthew 1:21 tell us that Jesus will save His people from their sins. In order to do that, Jesus had to become sin on our behalf. He literally became the sacrifice for sin. The Bible also informs us that Jesus became sickness so that we would not have to endure the debilitating effects of sickness and disease.

"But He was wounded for our transgressions, He was bruised for our iniquities; The chastisement for our peace was upon Him, And by His stripes we are healed" (Isa. 53:5).

Jesus' crisis involved having to go through unusual degrees of rejection and being betrayed by the people whom He loved the most. He was beaten with a cat-o-nine-tails and fastened to a wooden cross with nails. They lied about Jesus, abused Him, stole from Him, spat on Him, and then crucified Him. All of these things were crises beyond belief. Yet it was in the midst of these crises that the miracle of the resurrection occurred.

> *How God anointed Jesus of Nazareth with the Holy Spirit and with power, who went about doing good and healing all who were oppressed by the devil, for God was with Him. And we are witnesses of all things which He did both in the land of the Jews and in Jerusalem, whom they killed by hanging on a tree. Him God raised up on the third day, and showed Him openly, not to all the people, but to witnesses chosen before by God, even to us who ate and drank with Him after He arose from the dead* (Acts 10:38-41).

Imagine what your life would be like right now if the resurrection never happened. What if Jesus stayed in the grave, defeated? Forgive me—don't imagine that at all. That is a horrible thought. You and I both realize that if Jesus were never raised from the dead, then we would be utterly hopeless. Life would not have any real meaning, nor would it have substance.

IT'S WHEN YOU ARE IN THE CENTER OF YOUR CRISIS THAT GOD IS NOT VERY FAR AWAY. IN FACT, HE'S CLOSER THAN YOU THINK.

You must not forget that the miracle of Jesus being raised from the dead began with a crisis. My brother and my sister, if you are in a major or minor crisis, don't run. Please don't hide. Start looking up. Begin to look to God for help. Ask Him for deliverance. Don't be afraid ask for your miracle. Jesus is our perfect example that God is attracted to your crisis, so He may prove that He is strong and mighty in our midst. It's when you are in the center of your crisis that God is not very far away. In fact, He's closer than you think.

> *"I will lift up mine eyes unto the mountains: From whence shall my help come? My help cometh from Jehovah, Who made heaven and earth"* (Ps. 121:1-2, ASV).

CHAPTER THREE

Confusing The Wise

For you see your calling, brethren, that not many wise according to the flesh, not many mighty, not many noble, are called. But God has chosen the foolish things of the world to put to shame the wise, and God has chosen the weak things of the world to put to shame the things which are mighty; and the base things of the world and the things which are despised God has chosen, and the things which are not, to bring to nothing the things that are, that no flesh should glory in His presence. But of Him you are in Christ Jesus, who became for us wisdom from God— and righteousness and sanctification and redemption— that, as it is written, "He who glories, let him glory in the Lord" (1 Cor. 1:26-31).

This chapter is one that I feel the need to deal with quite straightforwardly. This area has been one of long debate among Christians. It is the area where God uses foolish methods to perform the miraculous. One of the things that most people who are ignorant to the miraculous fail to realize is that God does not use logical or normal methods to communicate His power. If He did it would be far too human and predictable. Many theologians agree that God was (past tense) a God of peculiar miracles. By this I mean that God used strange methods to perform miraculous acts in the Bible.

Most people believe that He did perform miracles by employing strange methods. However, some believe that He no longer uses unconventional ways anymore. There was a time when Jesus told his disciple Peter to go fishing and the first fish that you catch will have a gold coin in its mouth worth enough to pay both Peter's and Jesus' taxes. That seemed fine for them. No one really argues about the fact that it actually happened. But is it possible that you or I just might find a gold coin in the mouth of a fish today whose worth could immediately satisfy all of our debts? It happened then. So, why couldn't it happen today?

On another occasion, Jesus healed a blind man by using a spit-and-dirt concoction that He instantly whipped up. Using His own spittle and the dirt beneath His feet, He applied this fresh mix to the closed eyelids of a blind man. Surprisingly, this man, who had suffered with blindness since birth, was able to see clearly after he had washed the substance from his eyes. It truly happened then. My question is, can that happen today? Or, must we be forced to stick with the conventional methods of healing such as modern medicine, which does have its limitations?

The problem of choosing conventional methods over the unconventional has never been a problem with God. God has always taken the unusual paths to communicate His power. Again, most scholars will agree that the Bible is a book that very clearly displays God intentionally using means to perform miracles that were often contradictory to laws of nature and human reasoning. However, far too few believers today believe that God can use peculiar ways now.

This is one of the main reasons why so many churches fail to see the glory of God in their services. There are many churches within my city that have great choirs and song services. You could travel throughout the Bible belt in the southern states in America and find in many churches sound preaching and teaching about man's redemption. Within the past two decades, mega-churches have become an almost new phenomenon in America.

These "find everything you need mega-centers" that minister to the needs of thousands of people each week have fashioned themselves much like a Nordstrom's store, making the customer first and quality customer service its highest priority.

While I wholeheartedly believe that we need to minister to the needs of the people within our congregations, I too believe that in our desire to become user-friendly churches, we have totally overlooked some of the very obvious needs that our parishioners have. We have erected large buildings in which to worship. We've built family life centers equipped with gymnasiums, olympic-sized swimming pools, full-service fitness centers, and even movie theatres.

We have great entertainment for the whole family. Our churches have become a Chuck E. Cheese for children, and a high-tech social nightclub for the adult crowd. Please don't mistake me; there is nothing wrong with reaching out to people wherever they are. There is absolutely nothing wrong with making your ministry relevant in order to reach the masses. You must reach the lost at any cost. My problem is that I believe that we, the corporate Body, have forgotten the very reason why the Church exists to begin with. If you have forgotten the message, let me remind you of it. Jesus gave the vision statement for the Church.

THE UNIVERSAL CHURCH OF THE LORD JESUS CHRIST (TO WHICH ALL BORN-AGAIN SPIRIT-FILLED BELIEVERS BELONG) VISION STATEMENT

The Spirit of the Lord is upon Me, Because He has anointed Me To preach the gospel to the poor; He has sent Me to heal the brokenhearted, To proclaim liberty to the captives And recovery of sight to the blind, To set at liberty those who are oppressed; To proclaim the acceptable year of the Lord (Luke 4:18-19).

It is this vision from which Jesus has never veered or strayed. He still desires that we communicate and manifest miracles of healing and deliverance to the poor and brokenhearted. If we will just be honest, we will have to admit that we have not been doing this like He commanded, primarily because most Christians have become afraid of the criticisms that will inevitably come when one chooses to live the miraculous life. Sorry to say, there are no conventional ways to do it. It's either you choose to do it God's way, which will always be strange to the human mind, or don't do it at all. That choice is solely up to you.

HANDKERCHIEFS AND CLOTHS USED IN HEALING

Ever since I got saved, which was more than twenty-five years ago, I always believed God. That is one of the reasons why I believe that God has blessed my ministry and my family with such abundance. If God speaks to me, I am just going to obey God. No questions asked. There have been times when God specifically told me to pray over handkerchiefs and anoint them in the name of the Lord. He told me to send them to the people who were sick in their bodies. He told me to also make them available to people that will come to Great Faith Ministries. God said, "Have them sleep with the handkerchief underneath their faces. Tell others to place the cloth on the affected part of their body. I will heal them."

When God spoke these words to me, I didn't think that they were all that strange, particularly since I had a scripture to confirm that this method was one that proved to be effective already. God used the hands of Paul to work unusual miracles. The cloth that touched Paul's body was anointed with the power of God to literally heal the sick and drive demonic spirits out of people.

"Now God worked unusual miracles by the hands of Paul, so that even handkerchiefs or aprons were brought from his

*body to the sick, and the diseases left them and the evil spir-
its went out of them"* (Acts 19:11-12).

After reading this verse I immediately believed that if God
could use Paul, then surely He could use me also. Using this
method healed people because I obeyed God. So I did as the
Lord told me to do. The most amazing things began to happen
within my congregation. People, who had heeded the word that
the Lord gave to me concerning this, were healed of various diseases. God was using this as a test of obedience for an even
greater move of His power that was soon to come.

God, in times past, has always used foolish things to confuse
those who believe they are wise. Things that can be studied and
mastered in universities are not the things that God uses to
demonstrate His glory. If you can master it then it cannot be
God, for God cannot be mastered. Furthermore if you can fully
comprehend a miracle, then it cannot be from God. A real miracle cannot be understood. Real miracles always have a dynamic, a
certain characteristic that will point the receiver back to God and
not man.

GOD, IN TIMES PAST, HAS ALWAYS USED FOOLISH
THINGS TO CONFUSE THOSE WHO BELIEVE THEY
ARE WISE.

If I had the power to heal anyone with a handkerchief or any
other piece of material, then I would be a god. I am simply an
empty vessel that is always willing to be used by the Master. God
will use the least likely objects to perform great tasks. Is there
really any healing virtue in a piece of cloth? Surely not! However,
there is great healing power in the cloth that God anoints with
His oil.

The focus is not on the cloth, and neither is it on the man.
God has chosen various articles and objects such as wood, a

stone, and even the jawbone of an ass to use as the point of contact to produce miracles. His reasoning for choosing such seemingly insignificant items is the same now as it was then. God uses foolish, insignificant, and powerless things to confuse the people who continue to look for things that boast of power and might.

GOD USES FOOLISH, INSIGNIFICANT, AND POWERLESS THINGS TO CONFUSE THE PEOPLE WHO CONTINUE TO LOOK FOR THINGS THAT BOAST OF POWER AND MIGHT.

Consider a woman whose body is racked with cancer. Because there is no certainty in the opinions of medical doctors and because some of their advice has proven to be fatal in times past, she decides to believe that lying on a mere piece of cotton prayer cloth would be a better choice to bring on her healing. Miraculously and inexplicably, she gets healed of her cancer.

According to man's thinking and reasoning, this woman has believed in a very foolish thing. Chemotherapy has been the choice of medical practitioners for several decades now in treating cancer patients. Although many still died using this method of treatment, there are many who have survived. Because of those who survived, this method of treating cancer patients has become widely accepted, although the side effects can at times be worse than the cancer itself. But we've been taught that the wise thing to believe in is scheduling regular treatments.

We are also taught by our drug-crazed society that the foolish thing to believe is that a piece of cloth, prayed over by an anointed man of God, could possibly have healing properties within it. Both arguments have justifiable grounding. However, one side is strictly divine territory, and the divine is the only ground worthy of standing on. Despite what skeptics and critics may say, I choose to maintain that if God used strange and foolish things to get people healed and delivered before, surely He is still doing it now.

WHO WANTS TO BATHE IN A FILTHY RIVER?

*Now Naaman, commander of the army of the king of Syria, was a great and honorable man in the eyes of his master, because by him the Lord had given victory to Syria. He was also a mighty man of valor, **but** a leper. And the Syrians had gone out on raids, and had brought back captive a young girl from the land of Israel. She waited on Naaman's wife. Then she said to her mistress, "If only my master **were** with the prophet who is in Samaria! For he would heal him of his leprosy." And **Naaman** went in and told his master, saying, "Thus and thus said the girl who is from the land of Israel"*

*Then the king of Syria said, "Go now, and I will send a letter to the king of Israel." So he departed and took with him ten talents of silver, six thousand **shekels** of gold, and ten changes of clothing. Then he brought the letter to the king of Israel, which said, Now be advised, when this letter comes to you, that I have sent Naaman my servant to you, that you may heal him of his leprosy. And it happened, when the king of Israel read the letter, that he tore his clothes and said, "**Am I God, to kill and make alive,** that this man sends a man to me to heal him of his leprosy? Therefore please consider, and see how he seeks a quarrel with me."*

*So it was, when Elisha the man of God heard that the king of Israel had torn his clothes, that he sent to the king, saying, "Why have you torn your clothes? Please let him come to me, and he shall know that there is a prophet in Israel." Then Naaman went with his horses and chariot, and he stood at the door of Elisha's house. And Elisha sent a messenger to him, saying, "Go and wash in the Jordan seven times, and your flesh shall be restored to you, and **you shall*** *be clean." But Naaman became furious, and went away and said, "Indeed, I said to myself, 'He will surely come out to **me**, and stand and call on the name of the Lord his God, and wave his hand over the place, and heal the leprosy.' **Are** not the Abanah and the Pharpar, the rivers of Damascus, better than all the waters of Israel? Could I not wash in them and be clean?" So he turned and went away in a rage. And his servants came near and spoke to him, and said, "My father, **if** the prophet had told you **to do** something great, would you not have done **it**? How much more then, when he says to you, 'Wash, and be clean'?" So he went down and dipped seven times in the Jordan, according to the saying of the man of God; and his flesh was restored like the flesh of a little child, and he was clean* (2 Kings 5:1-14, emphasis added).*

These fourteen verses give clear details that justify why God chose to use a foolish command in order for Naaman to receive his healing. From studying this passage, Naaman reminds me in many ways of people today, who believe that they have it all together in life. Naaman was not just an ordinary kind of guy. Naaman's name literally means one who is pleasant. By this, we can immediately gather that he was a person who was well-liked by people. He was pleasant to be around. His very disposition made others feel pleasant themselves.

Vocationally, Naaman was a very successful Syrian general. He was held in high esteem and confidence by the king of Syria. He was perceived and honored by his fellow-countrymen as their deliverer. However, Naaman had a crisis—he was a leper. Leprosy, during this time, carried with it a tremendous stigma. People were officially ostracized and quarantined from the community when they were diagnosed with this sickness.

If that were to happen to Naaman, it would terminate his career, limit his influence, and ultimately render him inactive. This winning warrior could not live with any of these choices. His only option was to be healed, no matter what the costs. As I have showed you before, God's will is to heal. However, God will often heal people using the unconventional methods that are strange to us, yet very common for Him.

The storyline lets us know that his wife's servant, a Hebrew lady, referred Naaman to a prophet by the name of Elisha. She had witnessed this holy man of God perform miracles in Israel in times past, and knew that, if her master could only see this prophet, he would be healed from leprosy. Naaman was eventually connected to this prophet through the interaction between his king and the king of Israel. But when Naaman discovered the things he had to do in order to receive his healing, he became vexed in his spirit.

You must keep in mind that Naaman was a highly-ranked and respected leader. For him, it was common to have people who waited on him and executed his orders without delay. Because of his authority and reputation, he thought that the prophet would simply wave his hand over his body like a magic wand and he would be instantly healed. But it was not that simple. God wanted to use foolish things to confuse the wise. The prophet told Naaman to dip in the Jordan River seven times and only then would he receive his healing.

Of all the rivers that God could have chosen He chose the most foolish. The Jordan River was not only the dirtiest river, but it also carried with it a horrible stench. Instead of people being healed, one could very well contract a deadly bacterial infectious disease from this unclean river. Bathing in this filthy river should have exacerbated his leprosy, not made it better. This method was perhaps the most foolish method to get a leper healed. However, this was just the way that God intended for it to be.

What you must recognize is God's strategic plan in all of this. If the Jordan River were a river that was known for healing attributes then the river itself would get all the credit for healing Naaman. Multiple thousands of people each year visit the country of Jamaica, West Indies to bathe in their milk river mineral baths. These are hot spring wells that have healing elements within the waters. Most people who bathe in these waters give credit to the waters for their healing, not God. God will never share His glory with anyone, not even the waters that He created.

So God uses foolish things as a type of diversion. God intentionally uses things that normal thinking people would immediately cancel off as impossibility. Once you have concluded in your mind, "that there is no way" or "that's impossible" or "that's never been scientifically proven," or "it'll never work," then God has you exactly where He needs you. You are in the right position to receive your miracle from God. When it seems absolutely crazy and utterly ridiculous, then you will know that God is the One who is the real driving force behind everything.

WHEN IT SEEMS ABSOLUTELY CRAZY AND UTTERLY RIDICULOUS, THEN YOU WILL KNOW THAT GOD IS THE ONE WHO IS THE REAL DRIVING FORCE BEHIND EVERYTHING.

Naaman had to come to this realization for himself. I'm convinced that Naaman really did not want to dip in the river. I even believe that Naaman probably would not have wanted to dip in a clean river. This man was so accustomed to giving orders and commands, not receiving them. For Naaman to have to receive a command from someone whom he had never seen or had not been acquainted with was a humbling experience.

His entire life hinged on his ability to not only flow with the supernatural, but he also had to flow with the abnormal. For example, the prophet Elisha told Naaman that he had to dip not one but seven times in this filthy river. The number seven symbolizes the divine number of perfection. It is a number that also represents completion. More than that, seven symbolizes the day that God took His sabbatical rest.

From one perspective, God was saying to Naaman, "after you've dipped seven times in this filthy river, you will be able to receive not only your healing, but also rest." Rest from what you ask? Rest from the overwhelming responsibility of believing that he could do everything by himself. Most people that I meet desperately need this type of rest. All over my city and all throughout America people have been trying to do things that only God can do. As a result, they are now tired, worn out, stressed, sickly, diseased, and dying.

If Naaman dipped in the Jordan River five or even six times he would not have received his miracle. It had to be seven times. Why is that? God was doing with Naaman the same thing that He wants to do with you—break down your will. The principal way that He does this is by getting us to conform to His way of doing things regardless of how strange it may appear to be.

It is all a matter of submission to God. Far too many people think that they submit to God simply because they read their Bibles everyday, attend church regularly, fast and pray weekly, and give their tithes and offerings. God requires all of those things. However, if you have been a born-again believer for awhile, those things are more or less rudimentary for you. They are almost like rituals. Not to do those things would be abnormal to you.

What God is trying to get you to accept is that true submission will often involve a clashing of the wills, our will in diametric opposition to God's. True submission is when you will obey God by submitting and agreeing to do something that totally goes against the grain, something that you believe is simply imprudent. That is the place of brokenness. It is the place where God makes the miracle happen. That, my friend, is the place of your breakthrough.

WHAT'S SO STRANGE ABOUT SOAP?

Some years back my older sister began to lose great amounts of weight, rapidly and quite unexpectedly. The doctor tried various strategies to get her to eat and she refused. It was too painful for her to even eat. She was becoming, in many ways, incapacitated, unable to clean her house or properly bathe her body, much like cancer patients in their final stages of the disease.

In a short amount of time, she went from a size 16 to a size 6 in her clothing. It became increasingly apparent to me that my sister was dying right before my eyes. Since her symptoms were quite similar to cancer symptoms, I thought that she had cancer. Whatever it actually was, the doctors were unable to properly diagnose the sickness or find a cure for it.

I became really vexed about the whole situation. This was my sister and I have always dearly loved her. Seeking a solution to the matter, I prayed and asked God for an answer. I needed a clear answer, telling me exactly what I should do to aid in my sister's healing process. What God told me to do was far different than I would have initially thought. If God asked me to simply lay hands on my sister it would have been a normal request, and I would have responded without hesitation.

If God asked me to fast and pray for an entire week for her healing, without reservation I would have done it for my sister. Anything that God would have asked me that would have put me at a personal setback, disadvantage, or even inconvenience, I would have agreed, just to see my sister vibrant once again. God did not ask me to do any of those things. God spoke to me and told me to anoint a bar of soap, give it to her, and tell her to bathe with it.

His instructions were as simple as that. Following His order, I gave her the bar of anointed soap. My sister went home that night and washed her body with the soap. When she did something amazing happened to her. She fell out under the power of God in the shower, while the water was still running. When she got up out of the shower, her husband helped her to dry herself off, and put on her clothes. Totally exhausted, she went to sleep.

The following morning she woke up to her own surprise she was astounded to discover that her pain had totally left her. She wanted to test and see if this pain had truly disappeared. So she tried to do things that she could not normally do by herself. She began to wash, something she could not thoroughly do without assistance.

She started cleaning her entire house without anyone's assistance. Amazingly, she was able to eat a full course meal, something that she had not done in several weeks. In a short amount of time, she was down to a healthy and normal size, far smaller than she was before. God had used something as strange as an anointed bar of soap to heal my sister.

Although people have never intimidated me, I knew that when I obeyed God this time that I would open myself to enormous amounts of controversy and criticism. God was telling me to take this miracle public. He then told me to tell the people that if they would bathe with these bars of soap that miracles would indeed happen in their lives.

There may have been some skepticism if I only announced this to my church parishioners. That would have been enough to deal with. God was telling me to go on our national television broadcast, "Miracles Do Happen," and offer these bars to the general public. When I did what God told me to do I received more press from local papers and more talk within the church community than you would ever have imagined.

Quite frankly, I wasn't too astonished by the responses from the secular community. They are faithless. They do not know Christ personally and should not be expected to understand spiritual matters of faith in a way that believers understand. So any negative vibes from worldly folks would not have surprised me one bit.

My shock came from the Christian community, particularly senior pastors of well-established ministries. Several area pastors labeled me as a fraud and phony. For several weeks after that broadcast, I became the central theme of all of their messages. Sunday after Sunday they would get up in their pulpits and preach about why they thought that what God told me was not truly God speaking but rather another spirit speaking.

Several pastors told their parishioners that I was just like Simon the sorcerer who had bewitched the city. The unsaved people of the world were getting saved through these miracles. They found no reason to complain or to bring criticism against me. It was the church people that hurled false accusations against me. One would think that if people were getting saved and healed by the power of God at record numbers that it would be a cause for a celebration. Unfortunately, the religious leaders in my city did not see it that way.

> *Beware of false prophets, who come to you in sheep's cloth-ing, but inwardly they are ravenous wolves. You will know them by their fruits. Do men gather grapes from thorn bushes or figs from thistles? Even so, every good tree bears good fruit, but a bad tree bears bad fruit. A good tree can-not bear bad fruit, nor can a bad tree bear good fruit. Every tree that does not bear good fruit is cut down and thrown into the fire. Therefore by their fruits you will know them* (Matt. 7:15-20).

These leaders told their congregations to beware of false prophets. I too am a shepherd, whose primary responsibilities not only include feeding the sheep but also protecting them, making sure that they are safe. So I too would warn the people that I lead if I believed that someone was teaching false doctrine to them. But that was not the matter in this case.

What they all failed to realize from this text is that there were words that came after the, "Beware of false prophets, who come to you in sheep's clothing, but inwardly they are ravenous wolves." The one thing that drove me then and still drives me this day is the fruit that remains until now and that is exactly what came after the warning—"You will know them by their fruits." One thing about false prophets is that they cannot produce lasting fruit. Another thing that false prophets cannot do is bring attention to the glory of Jesus Christ, but rather to themselves. Those are major distinctions between false and real prophets of God.

THE MIRACLE OF WATER

If the criticism from earlier was not enough, far greater criticism came when God told me to pray over water. With that criticism was the greatest glory that has come upon our ministry. I remember the day ever so clearly, December 12, 1995. My wife and I had just suffered a major loss and our spirits were very low. It has never been my custom to sulk over any situation. I've always been able to control my emotions concerning loss. But this time my loss was a very personal loss for my wife and me. I knew that the best way to cope with my condition was to meditate on the Word of God. Scriptural meditation has always driven me to biblical success, and I knew that this time would be no different.

I was sitting in my office, meditating on this cold December day, trying to receive clarity about what had just happened to us. Also, I was seeking God's comfort. While I was meditating, the Lord spoke to me and told me to, "Pray over some water. When you do this and give it to the people, I will send major miracles in the lives of those who drink the water."

God specifically informed me not to sell the water. He also warned me that I should not take any credit for what He was going to do. Without reservation, I agreed to do as the Lord told me to do. At the same time, my housekeeper was very ill and could not even perform her work responsibilities like she normally would. I figured that I would use her as a sort of acid test to discover exactly what God was going to do with this miracle water.

I asked her to bring me a glass of water. When she did, I prayed over the water and then asked her to drink it. After she drank the water the power of God came over her so marvelously that she was immediately slain in the Spirit. When she finally got up, she was amazed at how she was totally healed by the power of God.

After this happened I brought this message to my congregation. The people began to bring water to the service with them. I prayed over hundreds of bottles of water. The grocery stores in Detroit were literally running out of stock as people were buying water by the thousands of gallons. People in my congregation were being healed of all kinds of sicknesses and diseases. As they got healed, they began bringing water to their sick relatives in the hospital. After they drank the water, their relatives were being released from the hospital and their doctor's care.

All kinds of diseases were cured by the power of Jesus through this miracle water. Several people whose cancer had fully metastasized through their body were suddenly and mysteriously cancer-free. One man drank this water and was healed from heart failure. One lady in particular had a cross eye since birth. She drank the water and the Lord healed her eye, straightening out her eye completely. The people that worked with her in her office were amazed by the power of God. Before that they were confirmed skeptics. They did not believe anything that had to do with that miracle stuff. After seeing the evidence right before them, they had no other choice but to turn around.

With people spreading the word in the community about what God was doing, it began to cause a whole lot of excitement and generated enormous amounts of interest. An investigative reporter came to the church service with cameras to report on the healings. He began to ask various people in the congregation about their healing to try to determine whether or not they received a genuine healing.

People gladly confessed that they were healed of cancers and heart disease. One person told the reporter how she suffered for more than a decade with sugar diabetes yet after she drank the water God healed her and her blood sugar levels were normal. The news broke so rapidly that nearly every newspaper in Detroit covered the story about "The Miracle Water." Seemingly overnight, everybody in Detroit knew about our ministry and the healing power of Jesus Christ. And people began to get saved by the thousands.

We really experienced an exponential increase in our services after major television shows began to report on the phenomena that were occurring. Reports were aired on such well-known stations as Black Entertainment Television and Ted Turner's CNN station. The response was so great that we had to host a special service at the COBO Hall in Detroit. People came from everywhere.

Although our ministry has always been known for miracles, signs, and wonders, the unusual results that came from the miracle water really branded us as a miracle ministry. The strange thing is that the unsaved were probably the ones that were most profoundly affected by these manifestations. Again, I received unprecedented criticism from the clergy in our city, worse than ever before. Pastors falsely labeled me. They told lies about me. But the Lord allowed me to understand that there are some who claim to know Him yet do not understand His grace.

THE SAME GRACE THAT BROUGHT SALVATION IS THAT SAME GRACE THAT WILL HEAL AND WORK MIRACLES IN PEOPLE LIVES.

It seems somewhat like an oxymoron for a believer to not understand God's grace when that is exactly how they were saved in the first place. I would probably venture to say that many people quickly forget about God's grace after He saves them. Always keep in mind that the same grace that brought salvation is that same grace that will heal and work miracles in people's lives.

No matter how many people criticized me, God was and still remains faithful. On the program there were several people who came forth to share their testimonies about how God had used a bar of soap (a foolish thing) to produce miracles in their lives. There were people who, after using the soap, were healed of persisting skin irritations and eczema.

One woman confessed that, when she went to the doctor, her blood sugar level decreased which, prior to using the soap, was typically "sky high." A gentleman informed us that his high blood pressure became normal after he washed. Others were relieved of insomnia. There were several people who came into unexpected money after they washed with the soap. Even I used the soap in an area where I had thinning hair, and my hair began to grow back. How did all of those things actually happen? I really don't know that answer. What I do know is that God uses foolish things to confuse the wise.

You may ask, doesn't all of that controversy and criticism make you want to play it safe? Don't you think it's better to remain on the down-low of things? Not at all! If you are going to ever make a positive impact for God in this world, you are going to have to settle in your heart that you will have to obey God no matter what. That settles it! Criticism only makes me want to do greater things for God and help more people than I already have.

IF GOD SPEAKS IT, HE WILL PERFORM IT.

Right now I am anxiously anticipating the next foolish thing that God will ask me to do. Will it be a handkerchief or a bar of soap or maybe even a glass of water? I really don't know the answer to that. God will probably ask me to do something that I have never done before. What I do know is that if God speaks it, He will perform it. And that is the only thing that truly concerns me.

And it shall come to pass...

The Next Move of God

*"And it shall come to pass afterward that I will pour out My Spirit on all flesh; Your sons and your daughters shall prophesy, Your old men shall dream dreams, Your young men shall see visions. And also on **My** menservants and on **My** maidservants I will pour out My Spirit in those days. And I will show wonders in the heavens and in the earth: Blood and fire and pillars of smoke. The sun shall be turned into darkness, And the moon into blood, Before the coming of the great and awesome day of the Lord. And it shall come to pass **That** whoever calls on the name of the Lord Shall be saved. For in Mount Zion and in Jerusalem there shall be deliverance, As the Lord has said, Among the remnant whom the Lord calls* (Joel 2:28-32, emphasis added).

There are two things that I love about this passage of scripture in the Book of Joel. The first thing I love is what the passage clearly says. Joel's prophecy speaks of a day that will come when God's Spirit will be poured out on all flesh. In this day, the gender barriers that still exist in the church will be removed. Women who are in ministry will be accepted as equals to their male counterparts.

No longer will men argue about whether or not a woman should be allowed to preach, as if a man can grant such an allowance anyhow. Women will lead great ministries for God and do mighty things as they have been doing already. However, in that day the same male ministers that previously condemned them will acknowledge them for their commendable efforts and spiritual service. In that day, small children will be taken far more seriously than they are right now. They won't be looked upon as merely little people whose main concern is child's play. They will prophesy the word of the Lord with boldness, conviction, and accuracy.

People who have always been viewed as servant class or those who perform the duties of slaves, as we see today in certain parts of sub-Saharan Africa and Brazil, will step up to their rightful place as ministry leaders, "My menservants and on My maidservants I will pour out My Spirit." Whereas in times past, they were considered the lowly of society, God will raise these least-likely people up as prophetic voices to boldly declare the word of the Lord to the nations of the industrialized world.

But what inspires me even more is what the text says that is not as apparent when you first read it. The areas that you have to use spiritual sense in order to understand are the parts within the scripture that give pertinent clues as to what we should expect in the coming move of God. "I will pour out My Spirit on all flesh" says far more than what we see at first glance in the Scriptures. "My spirit" and "all flesh" are two keys phrases that must be understood when trying to determine whom God will use in the last hour of history and how or to what extent they will be used.

Let's look at "My Spirit." According to the New Exhaustive Strong's Numbers and Concordance, the Hebrew word for "My Spirit" is ruwach. Ruwach is translated as wind, by resemblance breath. The context is that at the appointed time, God is going to begin breathing on His people. When God does this, it's going to create a windy effect. In other words, the way that God breathes will blow so forcefully that no one will be able to shelter his or her self from its turbulent influence. That is extremely important to know.

Since everyone will be affected by the wind of God in the last days, it is important for us to know some distinct details about the wind. Let's look at six essential characteristics of wind that will help us to have a more concrete understanding of what God is going to do, and how to identify His miraculous power at work.

SIX ESSENTIAL CHARACTERISTICS OF THE WIND

The wind is...

1. Air that sets things in motion

2. Strong

3. Fast moving

4. Changes direction without notice

5. Easily takes on a new scent

6. Invisible

The wind of God will be clearly identified because God is going to begin to set things in motion that were not previously in motion. We are going to begin to see things that we have never seen before. The Church as we now know it will no longer be relevant to the ever-changing and complex society that we live in. There will be a great shifting that will take place in this next move of God.

This will bother great numbers of people who are satisfied doing things the way they have always done them before. In order for God's kingdom to fully manifest itself, the Church, as we know it, has to die. That might be hard on your eyes just reading it. It may be far more difficult to accept when you actually experience it. In order for God's kingdom to be real to us, we have to willingly abandon our old traditions that have limited the power of God for centuries.

This will be a great challenge to the flesh since most people hate to change. In the same manner as the children of Israel, who became lovers of idols rather than of the true and living God, it appears that God has allowed His people today to engage in an unhealthy relationship with the ideology of "the Church" for hundreds of years. This ideology is equally as idolatrous as erecting a golden calf.

IN ORDER FOR GOD'S KINGDOM TO BE REAL TO US, WE HAVE TO WILLINGLY ABANDON OUR OLD TRADITIONS THAT HAVE LIMITED THE POWER OF GOD FOR CENTURIES.

The problem is that "the idea of church worship" is not as easily identified as an idol as a golden calf is. If a person erects an image of a golden calf for the purpose of worship it is quite obvious that the calf does not represent our God. However, church as we know it is not as easily identified as idolatrous since so many people worship the image of "what God used to do." You may have heard people say, "God moved mightily in the 60's, or 50's." Although they might not realize it, what they are really saying is that God is not capable of moving today.

Because there are so many people who wholeheartedly agree that God's Church needs to stay the same way that it's always been, it is very difficult for God to set new things in order. He will not do it progressively, but rather, quickly. The time is quickly coming where God's breath will set new Kingdom directives in order. It will happen so quickly you will not even realize it. And it will happen without your approval.

Those who have an unfailing loyalty to the Church in its old and ineffective state will be passed by in this next move of God. God is looking for men and women who are unafraid to confront evil, not only in the world but also within the Church. The only way that people will have the boldness of heart to be able to confront evil is when their allegiance is first to God and His holy Church, not church as usual. They will refuse to be a part of the status quo. And when God begins the motion, they will travel with God in the same motion.

We've seen similar instances of how God implanted new order in His Church in times past through the ministry of reformers such as John Wesley, Martin Luther, and John Calvin. The new reformers who will choose to flow in the way that God is blowing will be persecuted just like these great men were. The one thing that even the persecutors won't be able to understand is that the more they persecute, the more God will supernaturally cause provision to manifest and miracles to happen.

> *"Behold, I will do a new thing, Now it shall spring forth; Shall you not know it? I will even make a road in the wilderness **and** rivers in the desert"* (Isa. 43:19).

The next characteristic about God's wind is that it is strong. This is significant because you need to recognize that the spiritual battles that you will be confronted with in the last days will not be anything like the battles that you faced three or four decades ago. The spirit of anti-Christ has already been unleashed and will actively begin to influence governments, both on national and state levels, to change all laws and statues that support anything that closely resembles Christian values.

They know that the power of any government is based on whether or not they revere the true and living God. So ordinary people who love God will begin to do extraordinary things to influence governments toward righteousness. Although academic education does play a role in being influential within political arenas, God is going to impart in us His own influence and strength to accomplish things that we never thought we could possibly accomplish.

*For the weapons of our warfare **are** not carnal but mighty in God for pulling down strongholds, casting down arguments and every high thing that exalts itself against the knowledge of God, bringing every thought into captivity to the obedience of Christ, and being ready to punish all disobedience when your obedience is fulfilled (2 Cor. 10:4-6).*

Depending on what part of the world you live, you may have witnessed a major windstorm. Chicago has been dubbed the "windy city" for obvious reasons. And if you live there you'll feel the effects of the wind nearly every day. Then there are places in the southern part of the United States and especially in the tropical Atlantic where they experience major hurricanes, with winds blowing more than 75 miles per hour. When the wind blows in those regions, as it increases in its strength, the wind overtakes anything that is in its way: literally moving it out of the way.

Sometimes long-standing trees are destroyed. At times, roofs are destroyed in the midst of the storm. Doors come off hinges and windows are often blown out. Small debris and landscaping are usually the first areas to be destroyed by the force of the wind since they are not deeply rooted in the ground. The only things that will be able to stand are those things that are so firmly rooted that the wind cannot destroy it. When God's wind begins to move with strength, it will expose those who are really a part of His army and those who just wore the army gear yet never enlisted.

WHEN GOD'S WIND BEGINS TO MOVE WITH STRENGTH, IT WILL EXPOSE THOSE WHO ARE REALLY A PART OF HIS ARMY AND THOSE THAT JUST WORE THE ARMY GEAR YET NEVER ENLISTED.

The person who is truly connected to God has absolutely nothing to worry about. However, the person who persists in staying in their old dead traditional settings will be surprised when they discover that the move of God literally moved them out of the way. God is a consummate businessman. Because of that, He cannot afford to have any hindrances opposing His move. Anything that will oppose the fresh move of God is not only viewed as a deterrent but also as a parasite sucking the very life out of a much needed renewal in His Church. Before God stops His move, one that will ultimately benefit His people, He will simply move YOU out of the way. So goes the old adage, "If you can't win them, join them."

NEVER BE FOOLED INTO BELIEVING THAT GOD'S STRENGTH IS YOUR OWN NATURAL STRENGTH. SUCH A FOOLISH PRESUMPTION WILL ONLY CAUSE YOU TO BE OVERTAKEN BY THE STORM.

If you are like the [debris or beautiful landscaping that serve no greater] purpose than to make the ground look prettier, the need for your services will soon expire. God is looking for people who are so hungry to see people saved that they will go to extreme measures to accomplish that goal and not really care what they look like while they pursue that goal. Remember though, that every act of God is simply that, an act of His will. Never be fooled into believing that God's strength is your own natural strength. Such a foolish presumption will only cause you to be overtaken by the storm.

> *So he answered and said to me: "This is the word of the Lord to Zerubbabel: 'Not by might nor by power, but by My Spirit,' Says the Lord of hosts"* (Zech. 4:6).

In the same way that God's wind is strong it is also fast-moving. The very last words that Jesus spoke in the book of Revelation were found in Revelation 22:20-21: "He who testifies to these things says, 'Surely I am coming quickly.' Amen. Even so, come, Lord Jesus! The grace of our Lord Jesus Christ be with you all. Amen." Although the book of Revelation has a strong end-time message, one can use it in other applications and glean great wisdom. "Surely I am coming quickly" also gives us an indication of just how God will work in the last days.

The things that took years to produce will now only take months. Churches will start today and within one year's time they'll have more than 3,000 new disciples of Christ added to the Church. God will cause quick growth to occur in ministries. Believe me when I tell you that the growth will not be because of some man's or woman's greatness. It won't be because they have a television broadcast. Whether they can preach well or not won't make any difference at all.

THOSE WHO YOU THOUGHT WERE THE MOST LIKELY TO SUCCEED WILL PROBABLY NOT BE ELEVATED WHEN GOD'S WIND STARTS MOVING.

When God's wind starts to blow, you will witness many overnight success stories right before your eyes. They'll at least appear to be overnight success stories. The real truth is that God has some people covered until an appointed time when He desires to reveal them to the world. For now, they are in a kind of holding pattern, waiting to land safely. Those who you thought were the most likely to succeed will probably not be elevated when God's wind starts moving.

Very often, the people who are thought to be the most likely to succeed have a spirit of arrogance that, in time, will bring them down. God cannot use people like this, since they believe that they can do it without His help. On the other hand, the very ones that you thought would never make it in ministry will be the ones to excel beyond your imagination. A classic example of this is a fine young man by the name of pastor Myles McPherson, who leads a thriving congregation in San Diego, California.

Pastor McPherson is a former NFL football player who was traded by the Los Angeles Rams in the early 1980's. After a bout with drugs and other excesses that consume the lives of so many professional athletes, McPherson made a radical change, giving his life to God after being witnessed to by two of his believing teammates. Since 1986, he has been preaching and evangelizing, sharing with young people and athletes how God turned his life around and how God could do the same things for them, if they would only believe.

Only four and a half years ago, on February 27, 2000, after six weeks of fervent prayer, Pastor McPherson began The Rock. The Rock is the fastest growing ministry in the San Diego area. At its very first service The Rock had more than 3,000 people in attendance. They now minister to nearly 4,500 people each weekend. They have an annual budget of more than three million dollars. Recently, they have launched a campaign to raise money over and above their budget to purchase a facility for their church that now travels from one rented facility to another.

They received participation from ninety percent of their congregation, raising 15 million dollars over and above their regular annual budget. Many people are astounded at how quickly God has increased this ministry. There are hundreds of churches in the San Diego region that have not reached this level of success in forty to sixty years of ministry. Yet, within four years, The Rock is doing what many churches only consider to be a dream. They continue to do three things that they believe keep their ministry in a perpetual state of growth. Those three things are, (1) Evangelize, (2) Disciple, and then (3) Deploy.

Most people would have never thought that a former NFL star could have ever been used mightily by God to pastor a thriving church. Others can't figure out how this church continues to grow, even though they don't have a physical church building that they can call their home. Most pastors, particularly "old school" pastors, drill young ministers on the importance of securing a building when starting a new ministry.

They'll say, "Son, you need to find yourself a building or a nice storefront to get started. You're going to need a place that is permanent." Obviously, Pastor McPherson's experience challenges that whole train of thought. Much like the tabernacle of old that was a temporary place of worship for God to dwell in, this congregation has learned to maximize its potential by reaching people wherever they go. And, at each place, God supernaturally caused their growth to flourish.

Another example of God's work being accomplished quickly is Bishop T.D. Jakes, who has become well-known for his bestselling book, *Woman Thou Art Loosed*, which has sold more than 2.5 million copies worldwide. For many years, Jakes pastored a storefront ministry in West Virginia and struggled to attract more than 50 members. After the release of his book, God caused things to take off for him. His ministry began to grow rapidly.

God led Jakes to reestablish his ministry in May of 1996 in Dallas, Texas. Jakes brought 50 families with him from his small church in Smithers, West Virginia to begin The Potter's House. In less than one year, the church went from 50 families to more than 26,000 members, making it one of the strongest churches in the nation. Because God's anointing was so strong in that ministry, many people willfully chose to become a part of this thriving church, leaving their dead churches where God's power was not welcomed.

As a result of this, hundreds of churches that were not prepared and refused to flow with what God was doing in the now were forced to close their doors. This is only another example of what happens when God's wind begins blowing. It clearly displays how He redeems the time on our behalf, causing us to accomplish far more than we would have ever imagined in a short span of time. What seemed to have taken forever in times past will be done in a moment when God's Spirit begins to blow.

"See then that you walk circumspectly, not as fools but as wise, redeeming the time, because the days are evil" (Eph. 5:15-16).

The children of Israel are another example of how God's wind blows to produce quick and miraculous results. Slaves under Pharaoh's rulership, the children of Israel were deeply indebted to the Pharaoh yet within twenty-four hours they became completely debt free. God arranged a strategic plan to free the children of Israel from their indebtedness and cause the wealth and riches of the Egyptians to overtake them. In the same manner, God is going to quickly cause miracles of financial increase to come on the disadvantaged in the last days.

It won't be because of their financial savvy or business acumen. It will happen quickly only to bring glory to a miracle-working God. Please, my reader, don't misinterpret what I am saying. Just because the miracles are going to come, and they will come quickly, does not give you an excuse to be unprepared. In fact, if you believe that God is going to move in your life in that way, you need to begin the process of learning about finances and how to use money, rather than having money use you.

GOD, THROUGH HIS DIVINE POWER, WILL QUICKLY SEND INCREASE. HOWEVER, YOUR IGNORANCE OF WHAT TO DO WITH THAT QUICK MONEY WILL CAUSE THE MONEY TO LEAVE YOU QUICKLY.

God, through His divine power, will quickly send increase. However, your ignorance of what to do with that quick money will cause the money to leave you quickly. You don't necessarily need to earn a Harvard MBA to prepare yourself for this move of God. However, you do need to educate yourself on the fundamentals of money management. It will quickly come and stay with those who are ready to receive it. Take the advice of Jesus as He instructs believers from the lesson in the parable of the pounds. His advice is that we should be busy working diligently toward an expected goal until He returns.

> *"He said therefore, A certain nobleman went into a far country to receive for himself a kingdom, and to return. And he called his ten servants, and delivered them ten pounds, and said unto them, Occupy till I come"* (Luke 19:12-13, KJV).

The Next Move of God

Another notable characteristic of the wind is that it changes direction without any given notice. This is important to know because you will exhaust unnecessary amounts of energy if you continue to chase the wind, even if it's God's wind. It makes much better spiritual sense to chase after God rather than His wind. God is fixed, and when you chase after Him you are likely to find and catch Him.

When you chase the wind you become frustrated not only because the wind is so fast, but also because it changes its direction far too frequently to plot. Knowing this, you will have to be more like God. What I mean by that is that you need to become much like a permanent fixture. This does not mean that you should not be open to what the Holy Spirit is saying to you now. What I mean by a fixture is that you need to have a firm foundation in the fundamentals of the Christian faith.

One of the main things that will cause believers to miss the move of God is when strange teaching and false doctrines that cannot be substantiated by the word of God carry them away. Don't entertain false teachings! People who do are the kinds of people who jump on every boat that is traveling down the stream. They believe everything that they hear. Again, I am saying that you must be open to what God is doing in the now. However, if a person espouses a doctrine that appears to be questionable, don't quickly accept it.

Don't quickly reject it either. It may be that you have not heard about it because you have not been exposed to anything other than what you've been taught in your circles. To administer the acid test, ask yourself this question: Does this teaching ultimately lift up the name of Jesus and cause people to want to accept Jesus as Lord? If the answer to that question is yes, then receive it.

If the answer is no, then reject it. When you ask, do so with prayer and faith. Ask the Holy Spirit to guide you. The reason I am saying this is because much of our thought processes are governed by what we have been taught. What you have been taught is wonderful if it is applicable to God's Word. For example, you could have been reared in a church that vehemently opposes miracles.

So, if you grew up in that church, you will automatically be inclined to believe that miracles are not scriptural, even though they are. That's why I informed you to follow the voice of the Holy Spirit, because He will guide you into the truth that you should know. The strange doctrines that I am speaking of are those doctrines that do not exalt the name of Jesus, those that are in diametric opposition to His words. The apostle Paul made it clear that there are some teachings that we should not need to learn over again since they are basic principles of the faith.

> *Therefore, leaving the discussion of the elementary **principles** of Christ, let us go on to perfection, not laying again the foundation of repentance from dead works and of faith toward God, of the doctrine of baptisms, of laying on of hands, of resurrection of the dead, and of eternal judgment. And this we will do if God permits. For **it is** impossible for those who were once enlightened, and have tasted the heavenly gift, and have become partakers of the Holy Spirit, and have tasted the good word of God and the powers of the age to come, if they fall away, to renew them again to repentance, since they crucify again for themselves the Son of God, and put **Him** to an open shame.* (Heb. 6:1-6, emphasis added).

The Christian believer should not have to relearn repentance from dead works. Teaching a person about having faith in God is elementary. In other words, there are some things that we simply ought to know as born-again Christians. No one should be able to confuse us when it comes to scriptural doctrines, such as the laying on of hands, baptism in the Holy Spirit, and water baptism. We know that Jesus was crucified, buried, and resurrected on the third day. For that reason we preach Christ crucified. No one should be able to convince us otherwise.

> *But I have a few things against you, because you have there those who hold the doctrine of Balaam, who taught Balak to put a stumbling block before the children of Israel, to eat things sacrificed to idols, and to commit sexual immorality. Thus you also have those who hold the doctrine of the Nicolaitans, which thing I hate* (Rev. 2:14-15).

John the Revelator warned that if anyone teaches "the doctrine of Balaam" as if it were God's teaching, that they would become a stumbling block to the believer. Such doctrines only serve as a point of confusion, and God will hold it as an offense against them. The doctrines of Balaam were motivated by sheer greed and unrighteous gain. The same spirit exists today.

The doctrines that he taught were specifically intended to deter the children of Israel from their God. He taught them to eat things that were sacrificed to idols. Those doctrines were an affront to God who vehemently opposed idol worship. Also, he taught the children of Israel to commit sexual immorality, which was symbolic of spiritual fornication. Both then as well as in our modern era, people have worshiped gods to their own demise.

They have become satisfied with impersonal gods who cannot redeem them. Because of this, people have forgotten the basis of their Christian faith. And if they continue in that way, they will eventually become apostates, totally abandoning faith in Jesus Christ. As the wind begins to blow, you must be rooted and grounded in God's Word so that you will not be moved away from His presence.

Have you ever driven down the street near a mall where there are a number of different restaurants? When you open your car window, you will immediately smell the scent of great tasting food cooking and simmering on the grill. The smell makes you want to go and order some food from the menu. Although you have not actually gotten out of your car and physically walked into the restaurant, you have a good idea what is going on inside, because the blowing wind blew the fragrance of the grill into your car.

On the other hand, when you walk or drive past the city dump, the putrid smell of rotten flesh and toxic waste matter is most offensive. Once you've identified the odor, you try to drive past the smell as fast as you can, only to discover that the smell seems to be following you three miles down the highway. Again, the wind carries the smelly odor of the trash and refuse wherever it blows.

That is a distinct feature of the wind. It easily takes on a new scent. You may be wondering, how then can I recognize the fragrance that God is giving off? How will I know for sure that it is God's fragrance and not an odor coming from a foul spirit? I believe that the apostle Paul gives us a clear indication of this in his letter to the Corinthian church.

> *But thanks be to God, who always leads us in triumphal procession in Christ and through us spreads everywhere the fragrance of the knowledge of him. For we are to God the aroma of Christ among those who are being saved and those who are perishing. To the one we are the smell of death; to the other, the fragrance of life. And who is equal to such a task? Unlike so many, we do not peddle the word of God for profit. On the contrary, in Christ we speak before God with sincerity, like men sent from God.* (2 Cor. 2:14-17, NIV).

In this coming move of God, we will be used to spread the fragrance of the knowledge of Jesus Christ. Everywhere we go, we will carry God's scent, and people all over will immediately notice whose scent it actually is. To the people who are both unsaved and saved, we will give off a scent that represents life in Christ and His Word. To those who have chosen to reject Christ, our fragrance will be much like the smell of the city dump to them, the smell of perishing. Every person who has been chosen by God to carry His message will feel so honored that they will carry it whether or not they receive compensation. What a fragrance!

EVERY PERSON WHO HAS BEEN CHOSEN BY GOD TO CARRY HIS MESSAGE WILL FEEL SO HONORED THAT THEY WILL CARRY IT WHETHER OR NOT THEY RECEIVE COMPENSATION.

The final thing that I wish to mention about God's wind is that it is invisible. Why is this quality so important? Wind cannot be seen with the naked eye—only its effect can. Because it cannot be seen, it must be perceived by faith. In other words, God is going to move in this last day through believers who have faith to know that God is a miracle-working God.

This type of person will not need tons of documented evidence to validate an act of the Spirit. They'll know that it's God simply because of the outgrowth of fruit that will spawn from it. It is only at this point that God will get the glory that He not only deserves but for which He has also longed for far too long. Although you cannot see it, you will still know that the work that has been performed was work from the Lord. This lifestyle will be the kind that every believer will have to live if they expect to be used in the end-time move of God.

"For we walk by faith, not by sight" (2 Cor. 5:7).

> *For in it the righteousness of God is revealed from faith to faith; as it is written, "**The just shall live by faith**"* (Rom. 1:17, emphasis added).

> *"For since the creation of the world His invisible **attributes** are clearly seen, being understood by the things that are made, even His eternal power and Godhead, so that they are without excuse, because, although they knew God, they did not glorify **Him** as God, nor were thankful, but became futile in their thoughts, and their foolish hearts were darkened"* (Rom. 1:20-21, emphasis added).

WHAT ABOUT "ALL FLESH"?

Strong's Concordance gives a definition of the word flesh. Its Hebrew translation, *basar*, not only deals with flesh in its literal sense, but also includes the whole body or every body within the body. Metaphorically speaking, flesh speaks of the pudenda of a human, more commonly known as male and female genitalia. It is from these areas that life originates and produces after its kind.

The context seems to suggest that the kind of flesh that God desires to pour Himself into is the kind that has the ability to reproduce after its kind. God will no longer be satisfied with His power dwelling within one person to heal and deliver people from bondage. God will get pleasure when what He has gifted you with is imparted into people everywhere. In the coming move of God the focus will not be on one man or one woman. It will not be on "this" great healing evangelist or "that" renowned prophet. It will not even be centered on one great revival outpouring in one church or within a certain sect as in the days before.

The focus will be on the Body of Christ. The Body of Christ will be the ones showcasing the miraculous power and love of God. It won't have to be a planned event, a crusade, or a miracle service. You might just be strolling through Wal-Mart and notice someone who is confined to a wheelchair. Suddenly, the power of God will come over you, provoking you to pray for that person's healing, and amazingly, they will be totally healed. You will be amazed over and again how God heals through the most ordinary people.

This outpouring will be representative of the entire Body of Christ, not just a particular group within the Body. "All flesh" very obviously includes all people; both male and female, old and young, slave and free. Galatians 3:28-29 says, "There is neither Jew nor Greek, there is neither slave nor free, there is neither male nor female; for you are all one in Christ Jesus. And if you are Christ's, then you are Abraham's seed, and heirs according to the promise."

It also transcends all ethnic boundaries imposed by man. The whole purpose behind God pouring out His Spirit on all flesh is so that His Kingdom will once and for all be easily identified to the world of unbelievers. For many centuries, the Body of Christ has been divided, segregated, and separated because of very trifling issues. Because of our schisms, we have never appeared to the world to be one united body. We have proudly separated ourselves to distinguish us from those whom we do not desire to be like.

God will flow through whomever He so desires. The message that He is trying to get across is as much for the Church as it is for the world. That message is, "The blood of Jesus Christ is what makes us one." It is Christ's shed blood that unifies all believers throughout the world. The Church will no longer be a large group of people with an obscured identity.

When God begins to pour out His spirit on all flesh, the people through whom He will pour Himself will be so far from what we deem to be conventional. It won't be something that we are used to. However, you will know that it is from God if you are sensitive enough to recognize His Spirit. Succinctly put, when we get unified in the Body, the blessings of God and His miracles will begin to flow uninterrupted.

A Song of Ascents. Of David.

Behold, how good and how pleasant it is For brethren to dwell together in unity! It is like the precious oil upon the head, Running down on the beard, The beard of Aaron, Running down on the edge of his garments. It is like the dew of Hermon, Descending upon the mountains of Zion; For there the Lord commanded the blessing—Life forevermore (Ps. 133:1-3).

MIRACLES IN THE COSMOS

As the coming of our Lord nears, we should even expect to see miracles in the universe, which includes atmospheric changes. Joel's prophecy briefly deals with some of these changes. "And I will show wonders in the heavens and in the earth: Blood and fire and pillars of smoke. The sun shall be turned into darkness, And the moon into blood, Before the coming of the great and awesome day of the Lord" (Joel 2:30-31).

All of these occurrences will happen to turn people's attention toward the awesomeness of God. Think about it, if you were looking at the sun and suddenly it turned dark, wouldn't you know that God's power either allowed it or caused it to happen? If you were to see blood and fire and pillars of smoke in the heavenly realm, would not that leave a strong impression on your view about God's awesome power? I would hope that you would be far more convinced about God's miracle-working power from seeing these things.

Some scholars have taught that these happenings are only symbolisms and should not be taken literally. Whether these atmospheric changes are figurative or not is really not the central point. The real point is that these things will manifest in a way that every person will be able to recognize as a wondrous work of

God. Somehow, we will clearly know and accept that God's hand is moving in the environment.

We often get snow in Detroit during the winter months. Sometimes, the weather will drop down to the single digits. Most folks who live here either have become accustomed to the cold or may prefer this kind of weather. However, cold weather and snowy conditions are not familiar in places such as the southern and southwestern regions of the United States. Even recently, I read that Charlotte was hit heavily with a record 1½ feet of snow, beating its 1926 record by nearly a half foot of snow.

This past winter, sections of northern Kentucky were hit with a major ice storm that not only caused some to lose their lives, but also shut the entire state down for days. These areas do not normally receive this kind of weather, yet God can shift weather patterns at His will. People who live in relatively warmer climates that have experienced record-cold temperatures now have to purchase warmer outerwear, preparing for the possibility of cold weather for years to come. They have to make the necessary adjustments to survive the changes. In the same manner, millions of people in the Body of Christ will have to make the necessary changes in order to stay current with God.

God can employ many different methods to showcase His power. The use of the sun and the moon are just a small part of the options available to Him. The sun's purpose for thousands of years has always been to provide sunlight and warmth during the day. The moon's purpose is to provide light during the evening hours. Both of their purposes have not changed. Yet, when God begins to pour out His power on humanity, what used to serve a particular purpose may soon change.

Since the sun and moon are such constant fixtures, God uses them to convey a message that the spirit of traditionalism will have to bow to the new working of God. Although it used to be a certain way for so many years it won't be anymore. God will use the atmosphere to set the pace as an example of what He is going to do in the lives of His people. Get ready for the change.

CREATIVE MIRACLES; A FAMILIAR PLACE

*"So God created man in His **own** image; in the image of God He created him; male and female He created them"* (Gen. 1:27, emphasis added).

Finally, all of these things that I have mentioned will happen, and in many places are happening as we speak. While they are happening, God is going to perform creative miracles, as you have never seen before. Never forget that God is Creator. Creating is a natural and normal part of His character. Whatever has become conventional in the arena of miracles and healing will no longer be acceptable to God. God is looking for men and women who will really believe Him for the impossible.

GOD IS LOOKING FOR MEN AND WOMEN WHO WILL REALLY BELIEVE HIM FOR THE IMPOSSIBLE.

The common cold, or a higher-than-normal temperature, are things that could be treated with over-the-counter pharmaceuticals. Those things don't qualify as impossible situations for man. Back pains, arthritis, high blood pressure, diabetes, and mood swings are all treatable with man-made medicines. Because of that, they do not qualify as medical conditions that are impossible for humans to care for. Although all of these sicknesses are ones that have proven to be total annoyances and have the ability to impede normal progress in life, most of them can be totally eliminated by consciously making some gradual changes in your overall eating and exercise plan.

On the flip-side, there are many medical conditions of which no one has found a cure that we know of. For example, most people who regularly receive kidney dialysis treatment do so because they have either had one or more failing kidneys in their bodies. Most medical doctors will tell you that once you begin dialysis treatments three times weekly, you have to continue receiving treatments for as long as you live. The only hope of ever getting off of the dialysis treatment procedure is if somebody donates his or her kidney for a transplant surgery.

Even after a person has found someone to give them a kidney, it still has a chance of being rejected by the body into which it's been transplanted. Situations like these are ones where man's power and wisdom are limited, and only a miracle from God can permanently improve the situation. I believe that God is going to use ordinary people who are filled with His Spirit to perform creative miracles as He creates new kidneys to replace old failing ones in response to their faith and prayer.

While that may seem to be a bit radical, miracles like this will happen very regularly. People who have had their legs amputated from fighting in wars or from diabetes-related problems will witness the power of God that will literally grow their limbs back. You may think that this sounds a bit strange, and it does. Nonetheless, God will allow strange phenomenon to happen for His glory.

Jesus said:

Most assuredly, I say to you, he who believes in Me, the works that I do he will do also; and greater works than these he will do, because I go to My Father. And whatever you ask in My name, that I will do, that the Father may be glorified in the Son. If you ask anything in My name, I will do it (John 14:12-14).

MIRACLES OF MASS-CONVERSIONS

"And it shall come to pass that whoever calls on the name of the Lord shall be saved" (Joel 2:32a).

The greatest of all the miracles will always be when a person is born again. The time is quickly approaching when every person who calls on the name of Jesus will be saved. There will be people who are known throughout the world as notorious world dictators who will call on the name of the Lord and receive salvation. In many places, it is already beginning.

This is an area where the people who were least likely to desire salvation will be saved by the power of God. The folks that you never thought or believed could be saved will accept the work of Jesus and receive their salvation. **Your friends and family members, for whom you have prayed and fasted for many years, will begin to ask you everything that you know about the Lord Jesus. Movie stars, professional athletes, famous business tycoons, and pop stars who seemed to be at one time against Christianity, will willingly and wholeheartedly embrace THE NAME.**

On the foreign fields in many parts of Africa, South America, Russia, and China, thousands of people are hearing the message of Jesus and accepting Him as their Lord and Savior. The ministries of great missionary-evangelists such as Reinhart Bonkke, Mike Francen, Billy Graham, Morris Cerullo, and T.L. Osborn are eternal proof that millions of people are being saved at one time, after hearing the gospel message. To God be all glory and praise!

For those pastors who have an egocentric dilemma, the fruit from these last-day mass-miracle salvation crusades is going to cause great humility to come on them. They'll no longer brag about the hundreds of people who are joining their churches each week, especially when they discover that there are people on the mission field who are seeing hundreds of thousands of people come to Christ in one single service. **In those same services, blinded eyes will be opened, deaf ears will suddenly begin to hear, lame people will mysteriously begin walking, and dead people will be resurrected.**

For once in history the Scriptures will be fulfilled that make the bold claim that every knee will bow down to the name of the Lord. The kingdoms of this world will bow down to the Kingdom of our Lord. **Governments that have barred public worship of the Lord Jesus, Muslim countries, polytheistic cultures, and regions where satanic worship is freely practiced, will all bow down and confess that Jesus is Lord.**

As these things begin to happen, more and more people will see the value in becoming open to the message of Christ. No longer will believers have to labor, trying to convince people to believe in Jesus and accept Him into their lives. It will be as simple 1 +1 = 2. The word of God will be preached + the people receiving the Word that is being preached = billions of souls saved.

Therefore God also has highly exalted Him and given Him the name which is above every name, that at the name of Jesus every knee should bow, of those in heaven, and of those on earth, and of those under the earth, and that every tongue should confess that Jesus Christ is Lord, to the glory of God the Father (Phil. 2:9-11).

CHAPTER FIVE

Signs And Wonders

The old saints used to define signs and wonders as God giving us a sign that makes you wonder. That definition, as simplistic as it may sound, really has a lot of value to it. If God truly sends a sign, it will make you wonder exactly how He did it. Before you can come to a definite conclusion, you will be inclined to admit that only God could have caused it to happen.

AS LONG AS GOD HAS BEEN DEALING WITH HUMANITY, HE HAS ALWAYS USED SIGNS AND WONDERS TO DEAL WITH MAN'S HEART AND TO COMMUNICATE TO HIM JUST HOW GREAT HIS POWER REALLY IS.

All throughout the Scriptures, God uses signs and wonders to demonstrate the miraculous. The Pharaohs had magicians who performed magic and cast spells. No matter how hard they tried, no man then or today could ever replicate the things that God caused to happen in the earth among His people. For as long as God has been dealing with humanity, He has always used signs and wonders to deal with man's heart and to communicate to him just how great His power really is.

"And I will harden Pharaoh's heart, and multiply My signs and My wonders in the land of Egypt" (Exod. 7:3).

Not only did God use signs and wonders to operate on human's hardened hearts, but He also used signs and wonders as a tool of deliverance. The hands of Moses delivered the children of Israel when he parted the Red Sea with his staff. When God caused the sea to swallow up and drown the Egyptian army, it was not merely a victory, but a wondrous work of God.

> *"So the Lord brought us out of Egypt with a mighty hand and with an outstretched arm, with great terror and with signs and wonders"* (Deut. 26:8).

King Nebuchanezzar often acknowledged the greatness of God's signs and wonders. In stark contrast to the kingdoms of this earth that would inevitably end someday, God's kingdom has no end, but exists in a permanently continual state. King Nebuchadnezzer realized that even his own tenure, as king would someday come to a close. This was all the more reason why he recognized the distinction between his kingdom and the kingdom of our God.

> *Nebuchadnezzar the king, To all peoples, nations, and languages that dwell in all the earth: Peace be multiplied to you. I thought it good to declare the signs and wonders that the Most High God has worked for me. How great are His signs, And how mighty His wonders! His kingdom is an everlasting kingdom, And His dominion is from generation to generation* (Dan. 4:1-3).

For those who argue that signs and wonders are not needed to bring people to a point of decision, consider the words of Jesus Christ in John 4:48. "Then Jesus said to him, 'Unless you *people* see signs and wonders, you will by no means believe.'" Jesus makes it clear that there are some people who will not believe on the name of the Lord until they receive a sign and wonder. Based on this scripture, it is easy to conclude that signs and wonders will help to usher in the coming of our Lord, giving the believers an advantage to reap billions of souls for the Lord.

GETTING ACCUSTOMED
TO SIGNS AND WONDERS

The only way that we will ever be able to clearly identify who is false from who is real is by first knowing God. When you know who God is, you cannot be easily persuaded in the wrong direction. In the same way that an infant can easily recognize the voice of his or her mother and identify with the actual scent of the mother, every Christian should be able to know who God is and exactly how He operates.

THE ONLY WAY THAT WE WILL EVER BE ABLE TO CLEARLY IDENTIFY WHO IS FALSE FROM WHO IS REAL IS BY FIRST KNOWING GOD.

"For false christs and false prophets will rise and show great signs and wonders to deceive, if possible, even the elect" (Matt. 24:24).

Some people become very paranoid after reading this scripture. They are so afraid of accidentally following a false prophet. There are false prophets in the land. And yes, they do have the power and influence to lead sheep astray, even the matured sheep. But they can only do this if a person has a divided focus. If their focus is solely on the Lord Jesus Christ, then they cannot be fooled. However, if they have a partial focus on Christ and a partial focus on the systems of this world, they will eventually become deceived.

Secondly, you must become very accustomed to signs and wonders. It should not be a strange occurrence to witness a miraculous healing, to see God cause supernatural provision, or to watch God destroy your enemies. One of the reasons why the children of Israel continually flirted with other gods, which can be likened to following after false prophets, is because they were not accustomed to God's signs and wonders.

miracles do happen

I did not say that they did not experience God's supernatural supply and provision; I said that they refused to get accustomed to it. As soon as God delivered them from the hand of the enemy, they began to complain and ask God to do other things for them that really had no spiritual value. God was trying to get his children hooked on Him, but they were constantly worrying about their temporal needs and their outward image.

Miracles, signs, and wonders need to become a familiar place to you. If they are not, a false prophet will easily be able to come into your life and lead you astray by the wonders that he or she works. When you are accustomed to miracles, they are more of a naturally-expected occurrence in your life. You believe that they are supposed to happen and you live your life expecting them to occur.

WHEN YOU ARE ACCUSTOMED TO MIRACLES, THEY ARE MORE OF A NATURALLY-EXPECTED OCCURRENCE IN YOU LIFE.

There have been more people who have been led astray by so-called prophets and prophetesses than you can imagine. And the count is still rising. The reason why so many people are being led astray is simply because the people have not become familiar (in a positive sense) with the miraculous. For example, most people are very familiar with money, particularly bank-tellers and retail vendors. They handle thousands of dollars every day in varying denominations.

Most tellers and retailers are trained to instantly be able to identify a fraudulent 20, 50, or 100 dollar bill. To the untrained eye, all of the bills, both the real and the counterfeit, look exactly the same. But to the person who has become familiar with handling bills, there is a big difference. In the same manner, when believers become accustomed to life in the miraculous, they will know by the Spirit when an imposter has come on the scene.

They will instinctively identify them through discerning their spirit. And they will not be deceived.

> *"And Stephen, full of faith and power, did great wonders and signs among the people"* (Acts 6:8).

> *"And through the hands of the apostles many signs and wonders were done among the people. And they were all with one accord in Solomon's Porch"* (Acts 5:12).

My final comment here is that every believer needs to be actively involved in working miracles, signs, and wonders, accessing the hand of God. God has always intended that the gifts of the Spirit be demonstrated by His Body, not just a specialized group of people. Stephen, one of Jesus' disciples, used his faith to believe that he, like his Master, could perform wonders and signs.

GOD HAS ALWAYS INTENDED THAT THE GIFTS OF THE SPIRIT BE DEMONSTRATED BY HIS BODY, NOT JUST A SPECIALIZED GROUP OF PEOPLE.

The apostles too worked signs and wonders before the people. Imagine the kind of impact that you would make for the kingdom of God if you began to work these signs and wonders also. That is surely a way for you to make the miraculous a habit in your life. Just substitute your name in the place of Stephen's and read it out loud so you can envision what God actually desires for you to do. He did not only intend for Stephen to accomplish great signs and wonders, but He also desires for you to do the same.

"And [YOUR NAME], full of faith and power, did great wonders and signs among the people."

TESTIMONIES

Throughout my life and the course of my pastorate, there have been so many miracles that have occurred that I truthfully cannot remember each one. In many ways, miracles have become a type of lifestyle for me and for those who have been touched by our ministry. However, there are still many skeptics who insist that miracles, signs, and wonders are only a figment of a man's imagination. They contend that these paranormal experiences are, at best, grand illusions of what the recipient believes will happen.

Although many choose to ignore the experiences that God brings, few can ignore the testimonies of people who have actually come face-to-face with their own personal breaking point and yet lived to tell about it. Below, I have listed a powerful testimony that substantiates the whole concept of signs and wonders. This testimony is very much a sign and a wonder from the Lord.

Bible scholars may argue and debate long hours over whether or not something is accurately interpreted in the Scriptures. Through their training and expertise, they can verify places, times, dates, and characters in the Bible. They have set in place a system of being able to determine the authenticity of the Holy Scriptures. But there is one thing that no scholar of Hebrew or of the New Testament scriptures can legitimately argue, and that is your testimony. Your testimony is one of the only things that God has given you that cannot be contested.

YOUR TESTIMONY IS ONE OF THE ONLY THINGS THAT GOD HAS GIVEN YOU THAT CANNOT BE CONTESTED.

Your experience with God is not simply a theological experience; it is a personal one, well worth sharing. I am a firm believer that we are able to overcome all adversity in our lives by sharing our testimonies. Sharing your testimony does several things. First, it gives glory to God; He has made it possible for you to be an overcomer.

Second, sharing your testimony silences the devil. Although the devil is a liar, he knows what you endured since he is the one who tested you in many cases. He also knows that you survived since he tried various ways to kill you. Because of this, your testimony is one thing that the devil cannot steal from you. He becomes speechless and confused, knowing that what killed others did not kill you.

Third, your testimony encourages others. You would be amazed to discover how many people are going through some of the same things that you already lived through. They might not realize that there is actually hope. But when you give your testimony, it opens up the door of hope, allowing them to know that if God did it for you, that He will surely do it for them also.

JUST HEARING AND REHEARSING IN YOUR SPIRIT WHAT GOD BROUGHT YOU THROUGH WILL MAKE IT THAT MUCH EASIER AS YOU FACE NEW GIANTS IN YOUR LIFE.

Finally, your testimony encourages you. Often you encourage so many other people, yet at the end of the day you need encouragement yourself. Hearing the words of your own testimony is a well of strength and nourishment to your soul. Just hearing and rehearsing in your spirit what God brought you through will make it that much easier as you face new giants in your life.

Then I heard a loud voice saying in heaven, "Now salvation, and strength, and the kingdom of our God, and the power of His Christ have come, for the accuser of our brethren, who accused them before our God day and night, has been cast down. And they overcame him by the blood of the Lamb and by the word of their testimony, and they did not love their lives to the death" (Rev. 12:10-11).

THE STORY OF HENRY HASSEL

It was a hot summer in 1992 in Daytona Beach and Henry Hassel couldn't wait to get home to Detroit after working so hard for the past two semesters at school. Henry, a freshman basketball player at Bethune Cookman College in Daytona Beach, Florida had worked very hard, completing his first year of college. He was so excited about going home for the summer to see all of his family and friends. To earn some extra cash to go toward the car that he wanted, Henry got a summer job at President Tuxedos.

To look at Henry, one would never think that anything was going wrong in his physical body. For the most part, Henry looked like a picture of health. He was a good-looking, strapping 20-year-old. He was big and tall, about 6'9" and two hundred and thirty nine pounds, playing center position for his basketball team. Being an athlete, it was obvious that Henry did not lack proper exercise. He had an avaricious appetite for chicken, chips, and soda pop. His future looked very promising, and everything seemed to be looking upward, particularly his athletic career.

Like most college students, Henry needed a reliable car to get around. One day during that summer, he went to a local dealership to find a car that would meet his needs and fit into his budget. At one particular dealership, Henry had located the car that he knew would work fine, especially fitting for a college student's income. He went ahead and consummated the deal, completed the necessary paperwork, and gave the car salesman his deposit.

On June 26, 1992 he went to pick up his car. However, when Henry arrived at the dealership, his salesman had already gone out to get lunch. He was told that the salesman would be coming back relatively soon, so he decided to wait until he got back. Henry knew that everything was done and that it would be just a matter of time until he was driving home in his new car. While standing there, for totally unexplainable reasons, he started to feel strange feelings of numbness in his legs and arms. It was very strange to him, seeing that he had never felt like this before.

At first, he tried to ignore his feelings, thinking that they might just leave if he didn't pay much attention to them. The feelings became more pronounced. At that point, he tried to swallow and, in his own words, he confesses, "When I tried to swallow, it felt like a blood clot was going down my throat." He would later realize from the physicians that when that happens, death usually follows minutes later. He shared, "I began to feel so uncomfortable and faint that I had to leave the car dealership.

"My body felt so weird that I could not stay any longer and wait for this man; I had to get home. I was driving my sister's car. She had a stick shift. I remember shifting the gears and feeling more and more numb as I neared my house. I could hardly move. Although the dealership was a little less than ten miles away from my house, I don't even know how I actually made it home in one piece, considering how I was feeling that day."

When he arrived at the house, he went inside and immediately fell onto the door. The door kind of acted as a prop for him since he was losing the strength to stand up. Henry's sister was totally alarmed by his actions. Instinctively, she knew that something was wrong with her brother. She did not know what it was, but she did know that it was very bad. Realizing that Henry was unable to stand without assistance, and knowing how abnormal this was, she decided to take him directly to the hospital.

The first hospital that he went to did not really know what was wrong with him. They totally misdiagnosed him. They thought that he had the flu or something that was flu-related. Seeing that he was in a great amount of pain, they gave him some painkillers, believing that it would cure his condition. The pain became so intense that it nearly blinded him. Despite that, they sent him home at about three o'clock in the evening. Seven hours later, on that same day, he was rushed back into the hospital. There he stayed for the next three days, under close observation.

What they discovered was absolutely frightening. They discovered that there was no blood flowing into his kidneys, his liver, or his colon. They don't understand how he was still alive. Anatomically speaking, he should have been dead because of that alone. When they examined his liver, it appeared to be all dried up and deteriorated. They asked Henry if he was an alcoholic.

He was not. Even if he said that he was, the doctors concluded that he was far too young to have experienced these effects, which only a seasoned long-term drinker would have. His lungs looked like the lungs of a person in his late sixties who drank hard whiskey for the past thirty or forty years every day. Henry was just too young for all of that to have happened in his body.

All of his vital organs were dead, yet Henry was still alive. It defied medical sense and reasoning. That all alone was a miracle. The hospital were he was could not help him, and had to use the life-star helicopter to fly him to the University of Michigan Medical Center. By this time, his mother had arrived at the hospital. She couldn't ride with him in the helicopter because there wasn't enough room. Henry's mom, Delores, a woman of prayer, prayed all the way while driving in the car to the University of Michigan Medical Center.

Henry recalls, "I came home for the summer, thinking that I was going back for the fall semester. Little did I know how badly my body was damaged. My aorta tore in my stomach area. This caused a false blood channel. Blood was flowing to strange parts of my body. When I arrived at the hospital it was early Sunday morning. They immediately admitted me into the hospital.

"I was so weak I could hardly breathe. They would not even give me water to drink because they did not know what I had. They did not want to take any chances. Imagine that, I was so sick that even water could have brought about greater harm to my body. Going in, I thought that they would discover my problem, treat me, give me some pain pills for the road, and I would be on my way back to good health in just a couple of days. It turned out much differently than that. To my surprise, I wound up in the hospital for more than three months. I went in on June 26, 1992, and I came home on August 31, 1992."

Even after the three months, Henry had to go back after two or three days after his release because his condition was still worsening. He was on feeding tubes and could not eat any solid foods. The doctors told him that he would be confined to a wheelchair for the rest of his life, if he lived. Also, they had to remove a large part of his colon. While he was in the hospital over the three months they had to wait six weeks before they could do surgery on his heart, since they had done surgery on his stomach not long before that.

They knew that at least trying to do the surgery would be Henry's only hope. However, the surgeons said that it would be impossible for a person to have back-to-back surgeries like this. They gave him a zero to ten percent chance of pulling through this.

Miraculously, he survived the surgery. But it seemed as if one problem after another occurred. He had to go back to the hospital because the catheter in his chest got an infection. They seemed to have fixed that problem. Added to that, he also had a colostomy bag, a tube inside his chest, and a feeding tube. The physicians did the absolute best that they could do in saving his life. However, they knew that they could not do anymore than what they had already done.

They had to be honest with Henry and let him know what the real outlook on the future for his life was. In both a truthful and delicate manner, they informed him that he would have to wear the colostomy bag for the rest of his life. They said that he would never be able to feed himself. For the most part, he would be close to a vegetable. The doctors wanted Henry to accept this prognosis as best as he could.

From that point, Henry stayed in the hospital during the week, but they would allow him to go home for the weekends. That went on for a few weekends. The last surgery that he had was yet another miracle. That surgery allowed Henry to be able to get rid of the colostomy bag, something that the doctors never thought would happen. But God had already begun working in a mysterious way.

Even prior to that, when the paramedics were rushing him through the emergency room, the nurses in the ER said, even though he was completely unconscious, they overheard him clearly speaking in other tongues. Henry doesn't remember any of these things to this very day. His physical man was dying but his spiritual man was quite alive. It was this point, when his spirit took over his body, that I believe God began doing the needed surgery on Henry.

His mother retells the story as she remembers it:

"His sister was there when all of this happened. At the time, I was house-sitting for the bishop since he and his wife, pastor Beverly, were out of town. My daughter called me and told me what happened. At first, the doctors thought that Henry had an awful case of the flu. I thought that since he was able to drive home from the car dealership safely that he couldn't be all that bad. From the time that Henry was small he has never been an ill child.

"As quickly as I could, I got my things together and went straight to the hospital. When I saw my son, he didn't look like himself. It really looked as if a demon spirit was attacking him. When he went to the bathroom, I noticed that his gown was soiled with blood. They thought that it might be a bad case of hemorrhoids. Seeing that his overall condition was worsening, they decided to move him into the Intensive Care Unit. One negative sign after another began to give way and at that point, I knew that the doctors had misdiagnosed my boy.

"They had to transport him to another hospital that was more capable of caring for Henry. There wasn't room for me in the helicopter. I remember praying all the way to the hospital as I drove by car. Henry told me, 'Mom, I don't know what is wrong, but I'll sure be glad when it is over.' Come to find out, he had a bowel obstruction. He was shaking profusely. I knew by the Spirit of God that the enemy was trying to take him out. My brother, who is a pastor, began to curse the spirit of death off of him. We began to praise God for what we knew He was going to do in his life.

When we arrived at the hospital, they rushed him into a room to begin working on him. I tried to go with him, but I could hear the voice of the Holy Spirit saying, 'you have to stop here, but I am going on with him.' Hearing God's voice gave me a blessed assurance that everything was going to be all right. Henry was reared at Great Faith Ministries and had been well-taught by Bishop Wayne T. Jackson and pastor Beverly about praying in the Spirit.

"At Great Faith Ministries, we had become so well-trained to believe that God was a miracle-working God that we just knew that He was going to heal my son. I remember saying, 'If all my son needs is a miracle, then we have no problem, because God is a miracle working God.' On Sunday morning, Bishop was conducting Sunday morning worship services at the time. So I could not reach him to let him know exactly what was happening.

"My daughter and niece finally got in contact with Bishop Jackson, and the church immediately began to pray and intercede for my son. When Bishop Jackson dismissed service, several hundred of the saints from Great Faith came up to the hospital, interceding on my son's behalf. They literally flooded the hallways and corridors of that hospital praying in the Holy Ghost and casting out the spirit of death. The support from the members, combined with their prayerful attitude, brought some of the nurses and staff members to tears.

"When Bishop Jackson arrived, he told me, 'I don't know whether or not your son is going to live, I don't know. But one thing is for sure; God did tell me that He is going to get the glory out of this situation.' I was a bit discouraged when Bishop did not give me an affirmative answer about Henry. But, it began to dawn on me that this was a test for me. I had to stand on what I had learned about the miracle-working power of God that I had been taught for so many years.

"It was a Monday morning when Bishop prayed for Henry. Henry was swollen. He was opened from his groin up to his chest. He really looked as if he were going to die. Bishop spoke life into my son. He said these words, 'You shall live and not die to declare the works of the Lord.' When Bishop Jackson spoke those words, my son rose straight up, although he was still fully unconscious. Bishop began to tell him, 'no, no, no, lie back down son.'

"For almost one month, my son laid in a semi-comatose state, unconscious. But God miraculously delivered him. In many ways I view Henry in the same way as I see Lazarus, who Jesus raised from the dead. The doctors told him that he would not be able to have children. Defying all odds and medical accessments, he had two healthy boys of his own. He now spends his days as a day-trader, seizing every opportunity possible to give God all the praise for giving him life back.

"From May to January the doctors gave a hopeless out-look. Now, God has used his story to give hope to the hopeless. Everything that the doctors said, God used for His glory. There was a liver specialist from overseas who was absolutely amazed to see him eating food. He said that he was not the same person. They said that he would never gain weight. He wound up gaining so much weight that he had to go on a diet.

"This miracle was a sign of Jesus' love. It is a wonder of how God restored him back to his rightful place. The surgeons were humbled by this experience. They all gave glory to God. Since then, one of the doctors has become a Christian. No doctor took the glory! It was all God's doing."

"This was the Lord's doing; It is marvelous in our eyes" (Ps. 118:23).

CHAPTER SIX

Where Sin is Great, Grace is Greater ROMANS 6:15-17

Moreover the law entered that the offense might abound. But where sin abounded, grace abounded much more, so that as sin reigned in death, even so grace might reign through righteousness to eternal life through Jesus Christ our Lord (Rom. 5:20-21).

At one time, the city of Detroit had one of the highest crime rates in the whole country. When crime was at its all-time high, there were many churches that were making their great exodus from the city, heading toward the suburbs. Pastors and their parishioners grew increasingly tired and disgusted of having their automobiles stolen while they were in service worshipping God. Deacons and trustees became weary when they would open up the church for Wednesday night Bible study only to discover that the church's sound system had been stolen.

The members that God blessed to be able to live in desirable and upscale neighborhoods became progressively more fearful about bringing their families into the inner-city. They did not want to expose their children to the violence and drugs that were so obviously exposed and readily accessible. Some folks felt like they and their children should not have to see prostitutes and drug-dealing en route to service.

They simply had enough. They thought that they should move their churches to a more suburban scene, where the sin was not as clearly exposed. When all the other churches moved out, God kept me right in Detroit. Even when I had an opportunity to move our church to Southfield, God did not let the plans prosper. Out city was in a dismal state, and we could not leave it that way. We were commissioned by God to bring light to the darkness within our community. If we left, that could never have happened.

Added to that is the truth that sin is not regionalized, as some people childishly believe. Sin is no more present in Detroit than it is in Beverly Hills or in the state of Wyoming. By moving out to the suburbs, they were not moving to minimal sin areas. They were only moving to areas where certain sins such as car theft, drug use, and prostitution were more controlled than in Detroit. Not only was it more controlled; there were fewer incidences of each occurrence.

WHEREVER YOU SEE GREAT SINFUL ACTIONS, YOU WILL ALSO SEE A GREAT MANIFESTATION OF THE GRACE OF GOD.

In Detroit, the crimes were far more visible. That was the main reason that I knew Great Faith Ministries needed to stay in the city, right where all the crime and poverty was. Wherever you see great sinful actions, you will also see a great manifestation of the grace of God. That is where you will experience amazing miracles and marvelous conversions. God never shuts down because of sinners; He offers more of His grace. And wherever God's grace is flowing heavily is exactly where I want to be.

A CORRUPT EARTH—
THE NEED FOR GRACE

The earth also was corrupt before God, and the earth was filled with violence. So God looked upon the earth, and indeed it was corrupt; for all flesh had corrupted their way on the earth. And God said to Noah, "The end of all flesh has come before Me, for the earth is filled with violence through them; and behold, I will destroy them with the earth (Gen. 6:11-13).

Although Adam's sin of disobedience and lack of faith in God's Word was the original sin, the corruption in the earth had not come to its pinnacle until Noah's time. The Bible lets us know in Genesis that there was great corruption during Noah's day and great violence in the earth. But, what actually were the sins that they committed during those times? Aside from violence, the Scriptures give us the sin that God condemned.

*And as it was in the days of Noah, so it will be also in the days of the Son of Man: They ate, they drank, they married wives, they were given in marriage, until the day that Noah entered the ark, and the flood came and destroyed them all. Likewise as it was also in the days of Lot: They ate, they drank, they bought, they sold, they planted, they built; but on the day that Lot went out of Sodom it rained fire and brimstone from heaven and destroyed **them** all* (Luke 17:26-29, emphasis added).

The Bible says they ate and drank. They got married. As in the days of Lot, they also bought and sold. They planted things and reaped what they planted. They built buildings. What was so sinful about these things? At first glance it seems like this list is an innocent one. We see people every single day eating and drinking. People are always planning marriages. Downtown Detroit as well as the suburbs of Detroit seem to always have building construction going on. So what's so sinful about those things?

It is not the eating and drinking or marrying or building or planting that God has a problem with. It is the attitude of apathy toward Him that He is most concerned with. Many people tend to lose sight of God particularly when they get caught up in the day-to-day process of doing things, such as worrying about how they are going to live from day to day. They begin setting their sights on other things that have nothing to do with God.

America has become a prime example of living life in the fast lane. Many people are more concerned about getting raises on their jobs than getting a spiritual promotion. "Where am I going to live? What am I going to eat today? I have no idea what I am going to put on. I need more money." These trivial concerns tend to be on the top of most people's priority lists. The problem is that God tells people not to worry about any of these things. Jesus so articulately tells us why we should not be concerned with and focus on these things.

*Therefore I say to you, do not worry about your life, what you will eat or what you will drink; nor about your body, what you will put on. Is not life more than food and the body more than clothing? Look at the birds of the air, for they neither sow nor reap nor gather into barns; yet your heavenly Father feeds them. Are you not of more value than they? Which of you by worrying can add one cubit to his stature? So why do you worry about clothing? Consider the lilies of the field, how they grow: they neither toil nor spin; and yet I say to you that even Solomon in all his glory was not arrayed like one of these. Now if God so clothes the grass of the field, which today is, and tomorrow is thrown into the oven, **will He** not much more **clothe** you, O you of little faith? Therefore do not worry, saying, "What shall we eat?" or "What shall we drink" or "What shall we wear?" For after all these things the Gentiles seek.*

For your heavenly Father knows that you need all these things. But seek first the kingdom of God and His right- eousness, and all these things shall be added to you. There- fore do not worry about tomorrow, for tomorrow will worry about its own things. Sufficient for the day is its own trou- ble. (Matt. 6:25-34, emphasis added).

When we focus on the things that we desire in life, we lose our proper focus, which should be Christ. Having a nonchalant attitude about the kingdom of God will inevitably birth corrup- tion. When corruption is born, it usually grows out of control very fast. In Luke 17:26-29, Jesus forewarns us not to become so unconcerned about the kingdom of God that we worry more about things that the Gentiles worry about.

Anytime people have an improper focus in life, it will always cause important areas to decline. God is the one who makes sure that all of your needs are meet and that you are provided for in life. When you forget that, you will begin to do things that totally neglect Him, such as working eighteen-hour days, three and four jobs, all in the name of getting ahead in life. When you do this, you are putting His kingdom second and the system of this world in first place. No matter what way you look at it, that will always produce sin.

GOD IS THE ONE WHO MAKES SURE THAT ALL OF YOUR NEEDS ARE MEET AND THAT YOU ARE PRO- VIDED FOR IN LIFE.

The reason that produces sin is because you will not have time to spend with God. All of your time awake will be spent trying to enjoy life, purchasing things, planting, building, and looking for someone to marry. You should know that those things are already taken care of by your heavenly Father. In fact, most people who stress over those things are the ones that don't recognize that God is their Provider.

When Jesus said, "My grace is sufficient for you," (2 Cor. 12:9), He wanted you to understand that His sufficiency was far greater than what most people could ever imagine. His sufficiency extends into every area of your life, every area of human need. When you begin to believe that, you will see righteousness increase in the land, and miracles blossom.

GRACE: A LICENSE TO SIN?

What then? Shall we sin because we are not under law but under grace? Certainly not! Do you not know that to whom you present yourselves slaves to obey, you are that one's slaves whom you obey, whether of sin leading to death, or of obedience leading to righteousness? But God be thanked that though you were slaves of sin, yet you obeyed from the heart that form of doctrine to which you were delivered (Rom. 6:15-17).

Grace is the unwarranted love and favor of God toward mankind. It is love that we don't really deserve. It's simply a favor. You can neither earn grace nor can you work to obtain it. It is a free gift from God. Now let's bring balance to this. Just because grace is a gift and an unrestrained expression of God's love, it is not a license to sin.

GRACE IS THE UNWARRANTED LOVE AND FAVOR OF GOD TOWARD MANKIND.

Some people teach, and mistakenly believe that, because God gives us grace, we should not be responsible to consider our moral behavior. God still requires all of His children to live lifestyles that exemplify His holy character. "Speak to all the congregation of the children of Israel, and say to them: 'You shall be holy, for I the Lord your God am holy'" (Lev. 19:2). His requirement for His people has not changed today.

God still requires and expects His people to live holy lives. I realize that, for many readers, you may want to close the book at this point and choose another one to start reading. Holiness has become a very unpopular theme in our modern society. Everything seems to be right. There are no moral absolutes anymore. Same-sex marriages are condoned and upheld in some state systems.

Adulterers and fornicators are applauded for their wanton lifestyles. After all, most of the programs that are aired on television tend to sensationalize sin. They make sin very popular and inviting. The only problem with that is that Hollywood does not and should not set the standards for God's holy Church. In fact, we should be the ones who are setting the standards for the world. In every way, we should teach them how to live lifestyles that are pleasing to God and fruitful.

GOD'S GRACE GIVES YOU THE RIGHT TO BE RIGHTEOUS BECAUSE OF CHRIST'S SACRIFICE.

So don't believe God's grace gives you an allowance to do anything you feel big and bad enough to do. It does not. God's grace gives you the right to be righteous because of Christ's sacrifice. Jesus made the sacrifice on the cross. He was beaten. But your response to His suffering should be a yielded life. You should not want to participate in sin, knowing what He went through to redeem you, to bring you back to the Father. From this moment on, you must view grace as a license to live abundantly—the ZOE, God kind of life. The Word Zoe is a Greek word that literally means life or animated life. When used in the scriptures it typifies life in Christ. Life in Christ always equals abundance.

A PERSECUTOR OF
CHRISTIANS FINDS GRACE

You probably could not get much worse than being a person who intentionally persecutes Christian believers. Well before the Apostle Paul had his miraculous conversion, he terrorized the saints. The believers were very much afraid of Saul as he was called then, because of his death-threats against the followers of Jesus. He ignorantly thought that he was not doing anything wrong by killing the saints and intentionally trying to destroy the Church.

Saul was reared as a fundamentalist Jew, trained to destroy anything or anyone that opposed Hasidic Jewish faith. Saul did not know Jesus and viewed him as a threat to the establishment of Judaism. Because of that, Saul consciously intimidated the believers. Whoever made it known that they were a follower of Jesus' teaching would be subject to physical beatings, psychological mind games, and often death. The Bible describes scenes that depict Saul's urgency.

> *"As for Saul, he made havoc of the church, entering every house, and dragging off men and women, committing* **them** *to prison"* (Acts 8:3, emphasis added).

> *Then Saul, still breathing threats and murder against the disciples of the Lord, went to the high priest and asked letters from him to the synagogues of Damascus, so that if he found any who were of the Way, whether men or women, he might bring them bound to Jerusalem* (Acts 9:1-2).

One of the things that Saul did not really know is that God will not tolerate this kind of behavior for long. God will not allow His people to be taunted and tormented by the oppressor. God is the God of the oppressed. Saul winds up having an epiphany, one that would change his life forever. He comes face to face with the Spirit of the Lord Jesus Christ on a road called Damascus. The Bible tells us about a great light that shines in Saul's face.

The light was so great that it blinded his eyes. Jesus rebuked him for being so insensitive and harassing towards the people of the Way. From that experience, Paul instantly received the grace of God and immediately began preaching the message of Christ. As is customary in Hebrew culture, after one has had an encounter with God, Saul's name was changed to Paul. He was a great sinner, one guilty of shedding innocent blood. Yet after his conversion, God's grace washed away the remnant of his past.

Paul later went on to write nearly two-thirds of the New Testament. He conducted massive crusades and was perhaps the most influential person in helping to establish the early Church. His conversion is nothing less than a miracle. But, the point is that miracle conversion will only produce more miracle conversions. I am no apostle Paul, but I can relate to his experience. In many ways, I too have had a Damascus road experience.

My testimony and conversion surely qualify as a miracle. And because of that, I feel eternally obligated to help as many people within my community and all over the world experience the same kind of miracle that I received. That is why I love people so much. Sometimes I feel as if I am possessed with a spirit of love for the people. I could never understand how preachers become arrogant and untouchable once they have arrived at a certain level of ministry.

Every single day, I am humbled by the fact that God actually chose me to convey his precious message of unconditional love. He could have chosen many other people far more articulate, more academically trained, far more popular, and even wealthier than myself. But he chose to use an ex-drug addict to spread this message of love. Even as I pen these words I am compelled to love. You ask, "bishop, why do you feel such a compulsion to love?" My answer: "I have been forgiven of much."

*"Therefore I say to you, her sins, **which are** many, are forgiven, for she loved much. But to whom little is forgiven, **the same** loves little"* (Luke 7:47, emphasis added).

MIRACLES AMONG SINNERS

So He got into a boat, crossed over, and came to His own city. Then behold, they brought to Him a paralytic lying on a bed. When Jesus saw their faith, He said to the paralytic, "Son, be of good cheer; your sins are forgiven you." And at once some of the scribes said within themselves, "This Man blasphemes!" But Jesus, knowing their thoughts, said, "Why do you think evil in your hearts? For which is easier, to say, 'Your sins are forgiven you,' or to say, 'Arise and walk'? But that you may know that the Son of Man has power on earth to forgive sins"—then He said to the paralytic, "Arise, take up your bed, and go to your house." And he arose and departed to his house. Now when the multitudes saw it, they marveled and glorified God, who had given such power to men (Matt. 9:1-8, emphasis added).*

One of the strangest things that many traditional saints have not been able to comprehend is why God chooses to heal sinners. There are even times where God healed a sinner during a service and believing Christians were not healed. This topic tends to baffle the minds of many believers. Most believers believe that God is unfair. I mean, why would God heal a dirty old sinner over a righteous saint anyhow?

This question can be answered with three very legitimate observations. The first is that God is simply *a merciful God*. God is not prejudiced in any way. So, His mercy endures to all people and to all generations. God does not show partiality toward people who are in need. Anybody can be healed, whether a sinner or a saint, if they will only believe. Healing does belong exclusively to the children of God. But, what that implies is that God's children should know how to readily access healing when they need it.

If it belongs to them, then they should always know where to find it. The sinners do not always know where to look when they need a miracle in their lives. Some look to psychics and others look, to mediums as a means of getting their strength and enlightenment. For the most part, they simply have not recognized that God is their One True Source. This is something that every believer should know already. Sinners are often more open to the possibility of being healed. That's why they desperately search out so many different sources.

MANY DO NOT BELIEVE IN MIRACLES. THE BOTTOM LINE IS THAT IF YOU DON'T BELIEVE IN THEM THEN YOU WILL NEVER HAVE THEM.

Which brings me to my second point. God is a God that *responds to faith*. Many sinners release faith for healing, while some believers tend to doubt the promises of God. It's really a shame that there are so many Christians who really don't believe in healing. Many do not believe in miracles. The bottom line is that if you don't believe in them then you will never have them.

Many sinners have come to a point in life where they believe that they've come to their last option. When their families have given up on them, doctors have given them up to die, and friends have turned their back on them, they are left with no other choice but to believe God. Unfortunately, many Christians feel as if they are not in as desperate of a situation since they still have a relationship with the Lord. What they don't realize is that God wants them to have it all. And often sinners come to this reality sooner than some saints do.

People ask, "Why won't God just heal all of the sick people in India?" The answer is, when faith is released for healing, healing will happen. There have been thousands of people who were healed during miracle campaigns after hearing the word of faith preached. So it is not that God won't heal. He moves when faith is released. That is why it is imperative for believers to live by faith and walk by faith. Until we begin to release our faith, the sinner will continue to reap our harvests, simply because they believe and we don't.

The final reason is found in this scripture, "now when the multitudes saw it, they marveled and glorified God" (Matt. 9:8). God heals sinners because He knows that it will bring glory to His name. Christians often tend to hang out in the Christian cliques. By doing this, they never really make an impact on secular society. However, when God heals a sinner, that sinner will let other sinners know what God has done for them.

IT ALL BEGINS WITH A MIRACLE.

That will ultimately bring glory to the name of the Lord. On top of that, more likely than not, that sinner will be so grateful to God that they will give their lives to Him and become recruiters for the faith. It all begins with a miracle. Mercy, faith, and His glory are reasons why God heals the sinner. Interestingly enough, these are the same reasons why He heals the righteous also.

CHAPTER SEVEN

Shadows That Heal

And believers were increasingly added to the Lord, multi-
tudes of both men and women, so that they brought the sick
*out into the streets and laid **them** on beds and couches, that*
at least the shadow of Peter passing by might fall on some of
them (Acts 5:14-15, emphasis added).

Do you believe that it is possible for your shadow to heal
someone? I believe that with God all things are possible. Theologians have debated this scripture to try and determine
whether or not a shadow can actually heal someone. Most theologians have concluded that the people mentioned in this passage were hopeful well-wishers, but not recipients of the healing
power of God.

Quite naturally, a mere shadow cannot heal a person. A
shadow is nothing more than a shade or reflection cast upon the
surface of the body. Although it can be clearly seen, it does not
have any tangible components within it. Medical science has
never proven that there are any therapeutic attributes in a shadow.
Yet, in this text, we see zealous believers and some unbelievers
who were laid on beds and stretchers in the streets, believing that
Peter's very presence could heal them.

It is obvious that these sick people were either paralyzed or
crippled in some way, necessitating the use of beds. It was common for the rich to own beds of such high value. The poor could

not afford beds like these and just laid on the edge of the streets. Both the poor and the young were in this crowd of sick people, waiting to be healed through the Christ-centered ministry of the apostles.

Many theologians discount the possibility of Peter's shadow being able to heal these sick people since the Bible does not specifically say that the people were healed. For example, the Bible says in Acts 19:11-12, "Now God worked unusual miracles by the hands of Paul, so that even handkerchiefs or aprons were brought from his body to the sick, and the diseases left them and the evil spirits went out of them." The Bible says that when Paul used handkerchiefs from his body, diseases and evil sprits left the people.

Matthew 9:21-22 says, "For she said to herself, 'If only I may touch His garment, I shall be made well.' But Jesus turned around, and when He saw her He said, 'Be of good cheer, daughter; your faith has made you well.' And the woman was made well from that hour." Again, we see an instance where a woman who hemorrhaged uncontrollably was healed miraculously through the hem of Jesus' garment. Both scriptures clearly state that people were healed as a result of these strange occurrences.

Concerning Peter's shadow it appears to be a bit vague as to whether or not anyone was actually healed. Because of that, it is difficult to formulate a "doctrine of shadows." However, it is very difficult to totally ignore that this whole experience is mentioned in the Scriptures. Why is it here? It could be very possible that the people who believed that Peter's shadow could heal believed so because they had witnessed it before.

It is very possible that they saw another crippled person who had the good fortune of being able to walk into an apostolic shadow. You may say, "The Bible does not say that they were healed by Peter's shadow, so you cannot say that they actually were." That is true. But on the other hand, one cannot say that they were not healed since the scripture does not specifically say that they were not.

Whether they were or not stands to be questioned. But there is one thing that is very strong here. The very fact that the disciples actually believed that Peter's shadow could heal stands to be reckoned. Peter is one of the disciples whose faith was remarkably noted for great signs and wonders following. I believe that the major message in this text is one that will provoke the believer to take off the limits imposed by man's reasoning and believe that God will do the impossible.

This scripture is one of great possibilities if you can see into it by the Holy Spirit. God can use anything to bring glory to His Name. I believe that Christians have become too restricted in their faith and in their possibility-thinking. Is it possible for God to use spit as a healing solution to cure blinded eyes? How about the fringe of someone's clothing? Can that be the tool used to heal a hemorrhaging woman?

Washing in contaminated and bacteria-infected waters would only exacerbate preexisting sickened conditions. Yet, Namaan was commanded to wash in a filthy river. God once used Elijah to lie on top of a dead man, causing life to come back into his body. The children of Israel were sick, and their mysterious cure came when they heeded Moses' command to stare into the face of a serpent. The list can go on and on.

WHATEVER GOD TELLS YOU TO DO, NO MATTER HOW UNCONVENTIONAL IT MAY APPEAR TO BE, JUST DO IT.

My heart wants to encourage you to release yourself from all barriers. Whatever God tells you to do, no matter how unconventional it may appear to be, just do it. Perhaps when you begin to exercise your faith on a continual basis your shadow will begin to cause healing to happen. Even if, for some reason, your shadow never heals anyone, continue to obey God. Knowing that you are underneath His shadow will give you the power to overcome the greatest obstacles that life may ever present.

> *"He who dwells in the secret place of the Most High Shall abide under the shadow of the Almighty"* (Ps. 91:1).

CHAPTER EIGHT

Prepare For Persecution

"For this reason the Jews persecuted Jesus, and sought to kill Him, because He had done these things on the Sabbath" (John 5:16).

I've heard so many Christians from various reformations say, "I want to be just like Jesus." When people say that, it sounds so pious and holy. It makes you almost feel as if you are already like Him simply because you want to be. But I have found out that many people that say that they want to be like Jesus, really don't understand what they are saying. In fact, if most of them knew exactly what being like Jesus entailed, they would probably not volunteer so quickly.

NEARLY EVERYWHERE JESUS WENT HE SUFFERED GREAT PERSECUTION FROM THE PEOPLE.

It's true that Christ worked miracles, saved souls, and raised the dead. But aside from that, Jesus was known for being persecuted. Nearly everywhere Jesus went He suffered great persecution from the people. At times, there were people who appeared to be on His side, who would shortly thereafter turn against Him, joining the side of the persecutors. No matter where Jesus went, He knew that He would attract persecution from the people just for doing good.

Yes, and all who desire to live godly in Christ Jesus will suf-
fer persecution. But evil men and impostors will grow worse
and worse, deceiving and being deceived. But you must con-
tinue in the things which you have learned and been assured
of, knowing from whom you have learned them, and that
from childhood you have known the Holy Scriptures, which
are able to make you wise for salvation through faith which
is in Christ Jesus (2 Tim. 3:12-15).

Timothy made a very noteworthy point in declaring "all" that live godly in Christ will suffer persecution. When the Scripture says all, that is exactly what it means. That makes me wonder about people who have ministries that are highly visible and very large, yet people never have anything negative to say about them or their ministry. I would be awfully concerned if no one ever said anything negative about my wife, my family, Great Faith Ministries, or me.

Now I'm not saying that I'm just looking for people to criticize me and persecute me, as if I want them to do it. I am not a glutton for unnecessary punishment. But I do realize that something must be wrong if everybody is on my side. I've heard someone say before, "If you never come face to face with the devil it is probably because you are walking in the same direction with him." That is absolutely true.

Now Saul was consenting to his death. At that time a great
persecution arose against the church which was at
Jerusalem; and they were all scattered throughout the
regions of Judea and Samaria, except the apostles. And
*devout men carried **Stephen to his burial**, and made great*
lamentation over him. As for Saul, he made havoc of the
church, entering every house, and dragging off men and
women, committing them to prison. Therefore those who
were scattered went everywhere preaching the word. Then
Philip went down to the city of Samaria and preached
Christ to them. And the multitudes with one accord heeded

the things spoken by Philip, hearing and seeing the miracles
which he did. For unclean spirits, crying with a loud voice,
came out of many who were possessed; and many who were
paralyzed and lame were healed. And there was great joy in
that city (Acts 8:1-8, emphasis added).

Anytime you decide to impact lives for Jesus you will always
have the opposition of the devil, for obvious reasons. Let me
inform you that the devil is not really afraid of millions of unbelievers getting saved as long as they don't do anything of value
after they get saved. If they never cast out demons or heal the
sick, and boldly confront sin, satan really could not care less
about their ministry.

He will allow you to have a successful ministry as long as
you allow him to continue to perpetuate the cycle of sin, sickness, disease, and poverty. But as soon as you receive the revelation from God to do those things, he will consider you a threat
to his kingdom and immediately begin using as many people as
he possibly can to persecute you.

HE WILL ALLOW YOU TO HAVE A SUCCESSFUL MIN-
ISTRY AS LONG AS YOU ALLOW HIM TO CONTINUE TO
PERPETUATE THE CYCLE OF SIN, SICKNESS, DISEASE,
AND POVERTY.

One of the things that automatically goes hand in hand with
miracles is the persecution that will inevitably come from the
religious community. If your personality is timid or if you are a
person who easily cowers down when people falsely accuse you,
then the miracle ministry is not for you. You have to be prepared
for persecution. People will lie about you. They will mock you.
They will scandalize your name. They will even frame you.

But, through all their attempts to malign your name and
speak evil against you, you must emerge from the ashes of their

criticism as a conqueror. You must know from the very beginning that you are already a winner in Christ. Since you are not the one actually performing the miracle, you don't have to defend the miracle. You are only the conduit through which the power of Christ is transmitted. The power comes from God, through you, to the person whom you are praying for in faith. Your job is simple: believe God for miracles.

YOUR JOB IS SIMPLE: BELIEVE GOD FOR MIRACLES.

If you believe that God has called you to flow in the miraculous, there are three areas that you will have to be careful of. If you can conquer lies and criticism from these three areas then you will be approved. Beware of attacks from your family and friends, the religious, and the media. If you can master these three points of persecution, you will be fine. Everything else will be trivial in scope.

DEALING WITH FAMILY AND FRIENDS

> *And it shall be in **that** day that every prophet will be ashamed of his vision when he prophesies; they will not wear a robe of coarse hair to deceive. But he will say, "I am no prophet, I am a farmer; for a man taught me to keep cattle from my youth." And **one** will say to him, "What are these wounds between your arms?" Then he will answer, "**Those** with which I was wounded in the house of my friends"* (Zech. 13:4-6, emphasis added).

Those who know you best in the world are your close friends and family members. They live with you in the inner-circle of your life's experience. Most people would be fine if they only received criticisms from the world. But when it comes from those who are close, it hurts so badly. You have to become

150

immune to the negative things they say about you. If you don't, what they say will eventually immobilize you and ultimately detour your focus.

One of things that I have come to realize about family is that, in time, they will come around. Family members have familiar spirits, and usually fail to recognize the anointing of God on the lives of people they know so intimately. Don't force them to believe in you and the vision that God showed you. If you were to be honest, just a few years back you wouldn't have believed that God would be using you in the manner that He is. His vision for your life at one time overwhelmed you. So, you can only imagine just how unbelievable your claims may appear to them.

DEALING WITH
THE RELIGIOUS PEOPLE

When Jesus departed from there, two blind men followed Him, crying out and saying, "Son of David, have mercy on us!" And when He had come into the house, the blind men came to Him. And Jesus said to them, "Do you believe that I am able to do this?" They said to Him, "Yes, Lord." Then He touched their eyes, saying, "According to your faith let it be to you." And their eyes were opened. And Jesus sternly warned them, saying, "See that no one knows it." But when they had departed, they spread the news about Him in all that country. As they went out, behold, they brought to Him a man, mute and demon-possessed. And when the demon was cast out, the mute spoke. And the multitudes marveled, saying, "It was never seen like this in Israel!" But the Pharisees said, "He casts out demons by the ruler of the demons"(Matt. 9:27-34).

One thing that you will come to realize shortly after you receive Jesus is that not everyone who claims to know God really does know Him. To really know God does not mean that you will obey long lists of rules, but rather, that you will wholeheartedly ascribe to what He says in His Word. So, if God declares that miracles and healing are available to the believer, that declaration should be accepted as truth and acted upon.

REMEMBER, IF YOU CHOOSE TO BE INTIMIDATED BY THE RELIGIOUS PEOPLE, YOU HAVE GIVEN THEM MORE GLORY THAN GOD.

When you hear religious people coming against miracles, it is not only a sign of their ignorance and shallowness, but also of their gross lack of compassion toward mankind. They'll do everything within their power to tear you down and stop people from being healed and set free. You cannot focus on their efforts because it will only distract you from the higher purposes of God. The late brother Kenneth Hagin, Sr. adopted what I believe to be the best practice ever in dealing with religious people. When he would be challenged or confronted by religious people either face to face, through letters, or via television or radio broadcast, he simply chose not to respond at all. He believed, if he gave a response, that he would be lending his voice to theirs, helping them to destroy his work for Jesus. So, like Jesus did when he was accused, Hagin also opened not his mouth. I realize that both you and I are human. And sometimes our humanity may get in the way. We always feel the need to defend ourselves. When dealing with issues that God has already preordained, no defense is really necessary. The only thing that we should rightfully do is obey God. Remember, if you choose to be intimidated by the religious people, you have given them more glory than God. You have made them your god, the ones to whom you have pledged allegiance.

DEALING WITH THE MEDIA

"Woe to you when all men speak well of you, For so did their fathers to the false prophets" (Luke 6:26).

Jesus said these words. This is perhaps some of the greatest advice that Jesus ever gave. Beware when all people speak well of you. If everyone speaks well of you, then you may very well be a false prophet. One of the main things that the media does so well is build up personalities. Whether they report favorably on a particular ministry, or if you have a well-known broadcast, the media builds you up in the eyes of the general public.

HUMILITY HAS BEEN THE GUIDING FORCE BEHIND
MY SUCCESS IN MINISTRY.

What they do not tell you is that they build you up for one reason, to tear you down. Because of that, you cannot believe their hype. More than that, you cannot believe your own hype. Humility has been the guiding force behind my success in ministry. Although I fully realize that God is blessing our ministry and thousands of souls are being healed, saved, and set free from the powers of darkness, I fully realize that God could have chosen anyone else. So, it humbles me that He would have chosen me.

You must use wisdom at all times when you are in the face of the cameras. Cameras have the ability to be very deceptive. They tend to make people believe that they are greater than they are. Worse yet, I have seen ministers who were greatly anointed fall from their positions into sin because they believed that they were invincible. They thought that since they were on television, or regularly written about in the newspapers, they were flawless.

As a result of being deluded by the enemy, they refused to listen to the correction of their fathers in the Lord. And today, they merely subsist. If God tells you to go on television, then do it. If He did not tell you, then wait until He gives you the green light before you proceed. Only then will you be truly empowered to succeed. The key is continually humbling yourself before His presence. I do this through prayer and fasting. It's what delivered me from addictive behavior, and now it is what keeps me conquering every battle that I face in life.

POLITICALLY INCORRECT—
SPIRITUALLY CORRECT

> *For truly against Your holy Servant Jesus, whom You anointed, both Herod and Pontius Pilate, with the Gentiles and the people of Israel, were gathered together to do whatever Your hand and Your purpose determined before to be done. Now, Lord, look on their threats, and grant to Your servants that with all boldness they may speak Your word, by stretching out Your hand to heal, and that signs and wonders may be done through the name of Your holy Servant Jesus." And when they had prayed, the place where they were assembled together was shaken; and they were all filled with the Holy Spirit, and they spoke the word of God with boldness* (Acts 4:27-31).

> *Then Paul dwelt two whole years in his own rented house, and received all who came to him, preaching the kingdom of God and teaching the things which concern the Lord Jesus Christ with all confidence, no one forbidding him* (Acts 28:30-31).

You have to recognize that when you walk in the miraculous you instantly become a target for great criticism and controversy. Obeying God will often cause you to have to confront societal evils. Preachers are not politicians. That is not to say that a preacher cannot successfully lead in the political arena. What I am saying is that the call to ministry supersedes any earthly calling.

On issues that pertain to God's Word and are critical to maintaining the moral fabric of our society, we must choose the way of the Word, Jesus Christ. In dealing with issues such as gay

marriages, stem-cell research, and abortion, we must straightforwardly make our stand. What does this have to do with miracles?
When you stand for righteousness in an unrighteous world you
are going to come under attack. They'll attack your church, your
miracle ministry, and your walk with the Lord.

WHEN YOU STAND FOR RIGHTEOUSNESS IN AN
UNRIGHTEOUS WORLD YOU ARE GOING TO COME
UNDER ATTACK.

You must know that their attacks will only bring about a
greater, more intense anointing on your life. This will inevitably
produce more miracles and God will be glorified. Regarding
matters that are central to the orthodox Christian faith, you must
determine to stand boldly on the side of Christ. That is the only
position that will produce victory, time and again.

I'M DOING THIS FOR GOD, NOT MAN

Your motivation is not the motivation that worldly people
have. Worldly people do what they do so that they can receive the
praises and accolades of men. We, the believers, do what we do to
receive God's approval, not men's. Each time we pray for a person
to receive healing, strength, and financial resources, we are doing
it for the sake of Christ and His kingdom. In fact, that is how
Christians should interpret their behavior and daily choices.

The question that they should always ask is, "Does my
choice contribute to the sake of Christ and His kingdom? The
university that you choose to attend needs to somehow have the
ability to ultimately promote Christ and His kingdom. The
classes that you choose should do the same. The clothes that you
choose to wear should promote the cause of Christ. They should
reflect His regal nature.

Even the friends that you select should help to enhance Christ and His kingdom. The music that you listen to, the books that you read, the restaurants that you eat at, and the places that you choose to shop, should all play a role, however small, in advancing Christ and His kingdom. I don't mean to sound redundant, but I do mean to impress on you that everything that we do is all about Christ and His kingdom.

Knowing that will help you protect yourself from the opinions of man. Evangelist Mike Francen wrote a book entitled, *The Call of God Supercedes The Opinions of Man.* In his book, he deals with Joel's prophecy of God pouring out His Spirit in the last days. Francen points out that God declared that He would pour His Spirit on the women, young people, elderly people, and common people.

IF ANYONE IS EVER GOING TO DO GREAT THINGS FOR GOD, THEY FIRST MUST GET OVER THE OPINIONS AND LIMITATIONS THAT MEN HAVE PLACED ON THEM.

He lets them know that if anyone is ever going to do great things for God, they first must get over the opinions and limitations that men have placed on them. Just face the fact right now that you will never be good enough to qualify to be on everyone's team. You are on God's team and He is cheering for you. That should be all that really matters.

ALL OF JESUS' DISCIPLES WERE PERSECUTED

If you are really going to do things for God, expect to be persecuted. It comes with the territory. Expect to be rejected. And most of all, expect to be misunderstood. All of the disciples were persecuted. All of the patriarchal fathers were persecuted. Here is just an abridged listing of some key characters who endured persecution. After reading this list, just add yours to the count.

Moses

When Pharaoh heard of this matter, he sought to kill Moses. But Moses fled from the face of Pharaoh and dwelt in the land of Midian; and he sat down by a well (Exod. 2:15).

David

For I hear the slander of many; Fear is on every side; While they take counsel together against me, They scheme to take away my life (Ps. 31:13).

Elijah

As the Lord your God lives, there is no nation or kingdom where my master has not sent someone to hunt for you; and when they said, 'He is not here,' he took an oath from the kingdom or nation that they could not find you (1 Kings 18:10).

Micaiah

So the king of Israel said, "Take Micaiah, and return him to Amon the governor of the city and to Joash the king's son" (1 Kings 22:26).

Job

Are not mockers with me? And does not my eye dwell on their provocation? (Job 17:2).

The Prophets Who Were Murdered by Jezebel

For so it was, while Jezebel massacred the prophets of the Lord, that Obadiah had taken one hundred prophets and hidden them, fifty to a cave, and had fed them with bread and water (1 Kings 18:4).

Lot

And they said, "Stand back!" Then they said, "This one came in to stay here, and he keeps acting as a judge; now we will deal worse with you than with them." So they pressed hard against the man Lot, and came near to break down the door (Gen. 19:9).

Urijah

And they brought Urijah from Egypt and brought him to Jehoiakim the king, who killed him with the sword and cast his dead body into the graves of the common people (Jer. 26:23).

Peter and John

They seized Peter and John, and because it was evening, they put them in jail until the next day (Acts 4:3, NIV).

All of the Apostles at once

They arrested the apostles and put them in the public jail (Acts 5:18, NIV).

John the Revelator

I, John, both your brother and companion in the tribulation and kingdom and patience of Jesus Christ, was on the island that is called Patmos for the word of God and for the testimony of Jesus Christ (Rev. 1:9).

Early Followers of Jesus

His parents said these things because they feared the Jews, for the Jews had agreed already that if anyone confessed that He was Christ, he would be put out of the synagogue (John 9:22).

James, the brother of John

Then he killed James the brother of John with the sword (Acts 12:2).

Timothy

Know that our brother Timothy has been set free, with whom I shall see you if he comes shortly (Heb. 13:23).

[Add Your Name] _____ was persecuted for the sake of Christ and His Kingdom.

Then one of the elders answered, saying to me, "Who are these arrayed in white robes, and where did they come from?" And I said to him, "Sir, you know." So he said to me, "These are the ones who come out of the great tribulation, and washed their robes and made them white in the blood of the Lamb. Therefore they are before the throne of God, and serve Him day and night in His temple. And He who sits on the throne will dwell among them. They shall neither hunger anymore nor thirst anymore; the sun shall not strike them, nor any heat; for the Lamb who is in the midst of the throne will shepherd them and lead them to living fountains of waters. And God will wipe away every tear from their eyes." (Rev. 7:13-17).

CHAPTER NINE

Go Ahead;
Walk on the Water

And Peter answered Him and said, "Lord, if it is You, command me to come to You on the water." So He said, "Come." And when Peter had come down out of the boat, he walked on the water to go to Jesus (Matt. 14:28-29).

Most assuredly, I say to you, he who believes in Me, the works that I do he will do also; and greater works than these he will do, because I go to My Father. And whatever you ask in My name, that I will do, that the Father may be glorified in the Son. If you ask anything in My name, I will do it (John 14:12-14).

I trust that your appetite has been stimulated for an intimate relationship with God after reading this work. But, having been supplied so much information, you may ask the question, "Where do I go from here?" You now recognize just how real and how readily available miracles actually are. But knowing about miracles and believing that they are real are only the beginning. You have to take the next step, a step of faith, and begin to act on what you know about miracles.

One of the things that I have come to realize about stepping out in faith at first, and very often in the beginning stages, is that it can be a very frightening experience. The whole idea of just stepping out on nothing and believing that God will offer His support without having any physical evidence can be a very scary thought. However, the initial scare will not last very long. It wears off over a period of time after you have faithfully pursued God.

LIKE PETER, YOU HAVE TO MAKE UP IN YOUR MIND THAT YOU ARE JUST GOING TO DO THIS. YOU HAVE TO BELIEVE GOD FOR THE MIRACULOUS TO BECOME A PART OF YOUR LIFE. AND YOU HAVE TO SIMPLY STEP OUT OF THE BOAT AND BEGIN TO WALK ON WATER.

Like Peter, you have to make up in your mind that you are just going to do this. You have to believe God for the miraculous to become a part of your life. And you have to simply step out of the boat and begin to walk on water. In the past, I've heard preachers publicly criticize Peter the apostle, since Jesus referred to him as having "little faith." The truth of the matter is that Peter displayed great faith in Jesus, simply by attempting to walk on water in the first place.

The reason why Jesus referred to him as having "little faith" is because Peter began to focus but for a moment on his present circumstances instead of committing his full attention to Christ. That was only a temporary distraction, but Jesus does not give an allowance for His followers to be distracted, even for a moment. This verse does two things: 1. it shows how much one needs to focus on Christ at all times, and 2. it shows how full of grace God actually is. Even in our most challenging times, when we are not focused like we should be, His grace compensates for our failures. Thank God for His grace.

How many people do you personally know who have actually attempted to walk on the water? You probably do not know anyone. And if you do know someone who attempted to walk on water, they probably drowned. Peter believed in Jesus so strongly that he attempted to walk on the water. He tried. That's a whole lot more commendable than not trying at all. This is what I love so much about Peter—he would at least try.

And this is the kind of person whom God is desperately seeking in this final chapter of the Church. God is looking for some more people who will at least try. He is looking for people who will dare to believe Him for impossible things. He's searching out people who, through their faith, will defy the common expectations of society and travel supernaturally beyond the limitations of natural men. "What if I fail," you ask? So what! The question you should ask is, "What may just happen, what is actually possible if I try?" You will succeed with the help of the Lord! Do not give up. Remember, the people who give up easily after one or two failures are usually laden with a spirit of pride. They believe that they are the ones performing the miracles. In reality, you cannot fail by walking in the area of miracles because it is not you performing the work.

IN REALITY, YOU CANNOT FAIL BY WALKING IN THE AREA OF MIRACLES BECAUSE IT IS NOT YOU PERFORMING THE WORK.

God does the work. He is only using you as a vehicle through which His awesome power can be transmitted. So there is no need to take it personally. If it does not work at first, just get back up and try again.

This brings me to my first point concerning walking on the water. If you are going to walk on water and do the impossible for God, you are going to have to cultivate the Spirit of persistence. Having the Spirit of persistence says that you will never quit and that you have resolved to go forward despite any opposition. The bottom line is that you are going to continue on until you receive your desired results.

DOG-ON FAITH

"And she said, 'Yes, Lord, yet even the little dogs eat the crumbs which fall from their masters' table'" (Matt. 15:27).

Jesus often used natural examples to illustrate great spiritual truths. I would like to share such an example, in which my wife's dog literally taught me how to live by faith. Some years ago, my wife and I purchased an extremely rare thoroughbred dog imported from France. His name is Dynasty. When we purchased Dynasty, my wife was given a tall list of do's and don'ts and proper care guidelines for this uncommon canine.

On the list of don'ts was: Do not, under any circumstances, give the dog table food! Because this dog was a singular breed, it had a very adverse reaction to table food. The dog was under a strict diet. He had to eat a specific type of dog food and could not deviate from this meal plan if he were to maintain optimal health. Some of the adverse effects would promote nausea and vomiting in the dog. Knowing my soft heart for animals, my wife drilled me on this issue and continued to warn me not to give any table food to Dynasty.

I'll never forget this one time when Beverly was not around and Dynasty came up to the kitchen table while I was having a bite to eat. He looked at me with his cute and cuddly self and just kind of stared into my eyes as if he were trying to hypnotize me. Although I was trying to ignore him, he just would not stop looking square into my face. After the back-and-forth staring contest went on for a few minutes, he seemed to have won, as I noticed myself offering him a small piece of table food.

He ate that morsel of food like it was his first and his last bite of food. I tried to ignore him after that because I did not want to get caught and convicted by my wife, who had already laid down the law concerning this matter. Dynasty had his moment and was satisfied for that time. The only problem is that

164

he never forgot the one and only time that I secretly gave him some food.

Like clockwork, every single time that I sat down to eat after that time, he came and sat in the same spot and began the hypnotizing sessions until he had me in his hand [paw?]. There were times when I would not even give him anything, hoping that he would think that our contract had expired. No such chance with this dog. Whether I gave him a sample taste of my food or not, that did not matter. He showed up faithfully on time, at the right spot every single time, just like a sergeant in the United States Marines shows up to command his troops.

More often than not, I would give him what he was asking for despite the repercussion that I knew would inevitably follow from my wife. I took my chances because I felt within that this dog's faithfulness to keep on coming back, time after time, must be rewarded. In some ways, I felt as if I would be robbing the dog if I did not reward him for his faith-filled actions. The dog kept coming back because he believed that, after a while, I was going to reward him. Nothing in the world could change his mind about that, not even me holding back from him a time or two.

God began to speak to me through that situation. He said, "If this dog can have that much faith to believe that you will give him food that he really isn't supposed to be eating, how much more should you believe that I will supply all of your needs?" After I thought about it for a minute, it simply blew me away. My faith increased greater than ever before. I knew that God treasured me far more than he did a dog, even if it was my wife's dog. And if God will reward my dog's faithfulness, how much more will He reward me if I keep on coming?

So many believers get discouraged if they don't seem to get rewarded immediately. I've come to discover that God looks for and rewards persistent faith. It is that kind of faith that never seems to quit. God showed me a spiritual principle through Dynasty's example, which every believer should practice if they want to get Kingdom results. This dog showed up faithfully at the same place and at the same time, believing that he was going to receive his blessing.

> *Ask, and it will be given to you; seek, and you will find; knock, and it will be opened to you. For everyone who asks receives, and he who seeks finds, and to him who knocks it will be opened. Or what man is there among you who, if his son asks for bread, will give him a stone? Or if he asks for a fish, will he give him a serpent? If you then, being evil, know how to give good gifts to your children, how much more will your Father who is in heaven give good things to those who ask Him!* (Matt. 7:7-11)

What would happen if you began to show up every single day, week, or month at the same time and place and stare into the face of God, refusing to move out of that place until He blessed you? I think that God would be inclined to bless you beyond belief. He wouldn't have any other choice but to bless you because your persistent faith would literally draw His favor into your life.

God is trying to get the believer to become diligent in seeking Him. If most believers were as faithful in seeking God's face as they were in seeking other things, they would have all of those things and, better than that, they would have God. Unfortunately, most Christians have not learned the secret yet. Seek God first. Things will always follow. However if you faithfully seek the things, more than likely you won't get the things and you wind up with a whole lot of unnecessary grief.

> *But seek first the kingdom of God and His righteousness, and all these things shall be added to you. Therefore do not worry about tomorrow, for tomorrow will worry about its own things. Sufficient for the day is its own trouble* (Matt 6:33-34).

WALK ON WATER
IN THE AREA OF HEALING

You may have a friend who is terminally ill. This can be an opportunity for you to walk on the water and believe God for the impossible to occur in his or her life. You ask, "How can I move in the miraculous on his or her behalf?" You will have to do something that you have never done in order to get what you have never received. I know firsthand the power of fervent prayer. But I also know that prayer coupled with action produces supernatural results.

PRAYER COUPLED WITH ACTION PRODUCES SUPER-
NATURAL RESULTS.

I have a dear friend who was conducting a healing crusade at a small church in East Stroudsburg, Pennsylvania. The pastor of the church there informed the visiting evangelist that his sister was approaching the point of death. She had cancer in her body, and the cancer had metastasized so quickly that there was nothing more for the doctors to do. The pastor asked the evangelist to pray over a robe that his sister often wore around the house. He believed, by praying over the robe, that God would cause His anointing to flow into the material and then into her body once she put it on. He planned on bringing the robe to her home after the service.

The evangelist sensed within that this woman, who was too sick to even attend the service, needed a speedy miracle from the Lord. Otherwise, she would be dead within days, as the doctors had already informed her. The evangelist removed his jacket and put on the robe. The robe was obviously too tight for him, but that did not matter. He preached under the anointing and power of God. Then he proceeded to pray for the sick, and nearly every person who was prayed for was healed on that night by the power of God.

After the service was over, he took off the robe that was stretched out by his portly frame and gave it to the pastor. After the meeting was over the pastor personally delivered the robe to his dying sister. He told her what happened, and that she should simply wear the robe and God would heal her. Miraculously, God healed her of cancer. The method sounded strange, but it worked. There are many ministers who would have never done anything to appear so foolish. You cannot be concerned about how things are going to look.

IF GOD HAS CALLED YOU TO BE A WATER-WALKER, AND I'M SURE THAT HE HAS, YOU HAVE TO BE FAR MORE CONCERNED ABOUT THE RESULTS.

If God has called you to be a water-walker, and I'm sure that he has, you have to be far more concerned about the results. Did the preacher look strange, walking around preaching in a robe with lilac and yellow flowers on it? Of course he did. But did this woman, given a report of death with only a week, at best, to live, receive her healing? Of course she did. It never could have happened if he was afraid of walking on water and doing something different.

WALK ON WATER
IN THE AREA OF FINANCIAL INCREASE

There are countless stories of financial blessing within our church. In fact, I could write a book or two about the many financial miracle stories that have happened for our members. Of all the stories, one comes to mind about a single mother. This young lady has been a member of my church for eight years now. From the very beginning, she has always been a faithful church member, never missing a service unless it was an absolute emergency.

Over the years I would take notice of how she would volunteer for everything. She would clean the church and stay after church to ensure that everything was in perfect order, and she always showed genuine concern for my wife and my family's needs. Anytime there was a special offering taken, she would always be one of the first ones to give selflessly.

Unfortunately, she had lost her job. And as a result, she had fallen far behind on her rent and her landlord began the eviction process. On Sunday, she had sown a $300.00 seed into the offering, into my life. I did not even know that she had sown this money. Neither did I realize the magnitude of her dilemma. This was the last of all her funds. She knew that she would have to do something different in order to receive her miracle. That very same week, someone gave this faithful woman a home that had been newly and completely renovated complete with a new air-conditioning system, heating system, paint job, floors, and kitchen.

Furthermore, she received this house debt-free without any mortgage payments. Her title was free and clear. Imagine someone in the eviction process, ready to be thrown out on the streets, yet a few days later she becomes a homeowner. Now, she no longer has to be worried about being put out of her home, since she owes nothing on it! She honored the man of God, and because of that strange thing, she has inherited a supernatural financial miracle, much like the widow at Zarephath.

So she went away and did according to the word of Elijah; and she and he and her household ate for many days. The bin of flour was not used up, nor did the jar of oil run dry, according to the word of the Lord which He spoke by Elijah (1 Kings 17:15-16).

WALK ON WATER
IN THE AREA OF BUILDING

Pastors from all over the country are trying to build churches for God. Unfortunately, many of them are finding themselves in unnecessary debt and often putting the church in positions of foreclosure. They borrow money in the name of the church, at exorbitantly high interest rates. They sell bonds to members, with the hope of earning their bondholders a sufficient profit (as long as they continue to pay on time).

What many of them fail to recognize is that God can cause supernatural favor to come on men and women of God to build an edifice for Him just like He can heal a blind eye or cause the lame to walk. With God there is no difference. We recently dedicated our building in April of 2004. God, not man, allowed us to purchase our property with cash. We own two buildings on approximately 183,000 square feet, and the other is about 17,000 square feet, totaling 200,000 square feet of space.

The larger of the two buildings houses our sanctuary and executive headquarters. When we purchased the three-story building, which was formerly a Federal Department Store, it was a literal wasteland. Very few, if any, of the ministers in town saw the potential of this property. We began demolition on the interior structure, tearing down walls and floors, trying to get an idea of what might be possible for this property. General contractors informed us that, just to erect the sanctuary and the grand lobby, it would take anywhere from nine months up to year.

They also informed us that with all of the labor, materials, and licenses, it would cost us a least six million dollars to complete. As I was going to the bank to secure the loan for the funds, God stopped me in my tracks. He told me not to borrow the money. Instantly, I knew that God was preparing me for yet another miracle. I thought to myself, "If I don't borrow the money, how in the world will I begin the work?" I thought that was a legitimate question.

God told me to use what I had right before me. God literally said "whatever you need is in the house." With that word I began to ask various people within the congregation to pitch in and lend their skills and talents to help this project get started. I received an overwhelming response of volunteer laborers. Many of the brothers worked fifteen-hour days for the church, without pay. That alone is a miracle, I'm sure you'll agree. God allowed me to envision the architectural floor plan and convey it to the people who worked on the project. My wife became the interior designer.

Miraculously, we were able to begin worshiping in our completed sanctuary, with a grand lobby, in 59 days. That is absolutely unheard of in the construction industry. Just securing the proper permits for building would have taken close to two months alone. But God caused us to have favor with the building inspectors. And they were able to get our zoning allowance and licenses in record time. Even the people in the department of licenses and inspections could hardly believe what God did. And our building is debt free. We literally saved six million dollars!

It does not matter what area you are being challenged in. If you step out of the boat, God himself will lift you and give you the strength, the wisdom, and the resources to not only complete the course, but to also do it in record timing. You say you want your church to grow, you want your community to be safe, and you want to see people saved and delivered from the insanity of sin? It will never happen until you step out of the boat and, by faith, not flesh, walk on the water.

MIRACLES NEVER HAPPEN UNTIL YOU FIRST DO SOMETHING.

Stop looking to man's ability to get the job done. Nothing miraculous will ever be done by using your own power and strength. In fact, if you can do it, then you don't need the Lord. But if it seems far beyond your scope, you know IMPOSSIBLE, then it qualifies as an opportunity for God to show Himself strong. Remember, miracles never happen until you first do something. Not possible? Think again.

> *"But Jesus looked at them and said to them, 'With men this is impossible, but with God all things are possible'"* **(Matt. 19:26).**

MINISTRY CONTACT INFORMATION

You may contact Wayne T. Jackson by calling or writing the ministry at:

GREAT FAITH MINISTRIES INTERNATIONAL
10735 Grand River Avenue
Detroit, MI 48204
313-491-3900